TRAGEDY TO TRIUMPH

A Christian response to trials and suffering

FRANK RETIEF

Foreword by George Verwer

WO

Mil...
WORD AUSTRALIA
Kilsyth, Australia
WORD COMMUNICATIONS LTD
Vancouver, B.C., Canada
STRUIK CHRISTIAN BOOKS (PTY) LTD
Cape Town, South Africa
JOINT DISTRIBUTORS SINGAPORE –
ALBY COMMERCIAL ENTERPRISES PTE LTD
and
CAMPUS CRUSADE, ASIA LTD
PHILIPPINE CAMPUS CRUSADE FOR CHRIST
Quezon City, Philippines
CHRISTIAN MARKETING NEW ZEALAND LTD
Havelock North, New Zealand
JENSCO LTD
Hong Kong
SALVATION BOOK CENTRE
Malaysia

St James Church in Cape Town has manifested a mature and God-honouring response to their horrific crisis which is serving to advance the gospel of Jesus Christ, not only in South Africa, but around the world. Truly, God has chosen to put his people 'on display' (p. 87). The response of the church is in part the result of the 25-year Bible teaching ministry of Frank Retief.

With insight and conviction forged in the crucible of the vivid and painful corporate experience of St James Church, Frank Retief offers biblical answers to the questions every Christian asks when suffering occurs. *Tragedy to Triumph* serves as a primer on the biblical response every believer should pursue as the purposes of our sovereign God are worked out in the events and relationships of life.

John MacArthur

I have long maintained that the Christian world needs a theology of suffering more than a theology of recovery. We tend to focus on making life work as we want it to rather than on finding God more deeply in the midst of tragedy. Out of terrible suffering—the kind that none of us is promised to escape—Frank Retief passionately and practically shows us the way through suffering to an even stronger dependence on God and His Word. Crucial reading for all who face life honestly.

Dr Lawrence J Crabb, Institute of Biblical Counselling

Most pastors have preached on the mysteries of good and evil, but Frank Retief's *Tragedy to Triumph* is unique. It was born in the aftermath of the vicious, murderous attack on his congregation as they worshipped.

. . . The result is teaching that glows with a special intensity and relevance from which we can all derive great benefit.

D. Stuart Brisco, Elmbrook Church

In *Tragedy to Triumph*, Retief does what he is so good at. He resists the temptation to be novel and takes ancient truths and with unusual skill, applies them to the heartache of his people. In doing so he leaves us with a classic book on pastoral theology.

Tony Sargent, Worthing Tabernacle

TRAGEDY TO TRIUMPH

TRAGEDY TO TRIUMPH

Published jointly by Nelson word Ltd., Milton Keynes and Struik
Christian Books, Ltd., Cape Town, 1994.

ISBN 0-85009-636-7   (South Africa ISBN 1-86823-172-0)
(Australia ISBN 1-86258-313-7)

Scripture references are from the Holy Bible, New International
Version, copyright © 1973, 1978, 1984 by International Bible Society.

Cover photograph of Table Mountain by Thiel

Reproduced, printed and bound in Great Britain fro Nelson Word
Ltd. and Struik Christian Books Ltd., by Cox and Wyman Ltd.,
Reding.

94 95 96 97 / 10 9 8 7 6 5 4 3 2

Contents

Foreword

As I read the manuscript of this powerful book, my heart was gripped and challenged. It is a book that must be read by as many people as possible. The Holy Spirit will use it to blow away the unreality and superficiality that so pervades our society today.

Frank Retief is a man of great faith and great vision. Only four weeks before the massacre, Frank and I sat together in the coffee bar in the church sharing about the work of God and especially our mutual vision for world evangelism. Teams from our ship Doulos, which was under repair in Cape Town, had been ministering at the church and Frank felt they were making some giant steps as far as their own mission vision. When I preached at the church the next Sunday morning, I felt deeply burdened to speak from 2 Corinthians 4 about how God allows great suffering and trials to come on His people. Little did we realise what was about to happen.

Sometimes, even as Christians, we tend to want to bury our heads in the sand and pretend that things like this don't happen. This book is going to jolt many of us into greater faith, courage and reality. When we read about suffering in our papers, or see it on television, it somehow will all become a little more real. Above all, we will realise that there is something we can do in response. The awful events of suffering and death at St James' do not even represent a tenth of a percent of the horrendous suffering that has gone on around the world in the past year. It is my prayer that this book will help us face the real world in which we live and in turn, be more courageous as we go forward in prayer and action to change the world and bring people into a knowledge of Christ.

I hope and pray that this unique book will also be used to mobilise prayer for South Africa which is still at a great crossroads. Terrorism and killings continue, and if things get out of control, there could come a bloodbath as has been seen in many other parts of Africa. It makes us more aware that there is no real long-term hope and peace outside the Lord Jesus Christ.

This is not just a book of history and biblical theology, but it is a practical guide to reality and survival for all of us here on this fallen planet. It hits hard at some of the 'quick fix' answers that some people are trying to give us in these days and presents a realistic and biblical worldview that causes us to fall down and worship God in the midst of all the mystery. I hope you will not only read this book prayerfully, but also be involved in distributing it to others because it is one of the most badly needed messages for the church and God's people right around the world. Let's pray that it will go into many other languages and touch millions of lives.

George Verwer

Introduction

On the evening of 25 July 1993, the service at the St James Church in the quiet suburb of Kenilworth in Cape Town was rudely disrupted. A group of armed men burst through the door, fired on the congregation and threw hand grenades attached to tins of nails into their midst. As a result 11 people died and 55 were injured, some horribly maimed for life. This book was written in the immediate aftermath of that terrible event. In the ensuing confusion, hurt and pain, my colleagues and I attempted to articulate our thoughts as we tried to minister to our congregation. We soon discovered that we were speaking not only to our own congregation, but in fact to the whole country as the media turned its spotlight on us. In retrospect, we often wished we had expressed things better than we had or done something differently. Likewise with this book. It would have benefited had there been more time for reflection and hindsight. However, the violence here and abroad and the ongoing interest in the attack on a crowd of worshippers has not only kept the matter alive in this country but has also made it imperative that the response to the incident be made immediately. In spite of the fact that the congregation have tried to put the tragedy behind them and move on, the media insist on keeping it alive. At the time of writing only one arrest has been made and the youth concerned is still to appear on trial. Thus the matter constantly resurfaces in the newspapers.

In the light of all this, a few comments are in order. Firstly, this book is not primarily about the massacre on the St James Church. Rather it is a series of reflections on the lessons we, as a congregation, struggled to learn about

sorrow and tragedy. Certainly it uses the massacre as a
backdrop because that was our peculiar experience. I recognise, however, that tragedy can have many faces. In this
book I am simply using our own tragedy to extract lessons that are, I believe, universally applicable. Secondly,
from the outset we tried to make it plain to the press that
the loss of life and the terrible injuries inflicted on our
congregation were in essence no different from the experience of many South Africans living in the violence in the
townships of our land.

Since the attack on our church, several other massa-
cres have taken place in South Africa. Not only that, but
the ongoing conflict in Bosnia, Ireland, the Middle East
and Somalia far outweighs the St James massacre in sheer
horror, brutality and the number of people affected. We
do not believe we are the only sufferers in the world or
that our sufferings were worse than those of others, but a
number of elements added to the atrocity committed
against us. Our congregation is a multiracial one that
worships happily together. As an evangelical church, we
are concerned that the gospel should reach as many people as possible and our services reflect this urgency. In
addition we have a strong social upliftment programme
among underprivileged people, many of whom came to
sit with us in mute sorrow the day after the attack.

Another element that added to the tragedy was the
fact that our congregation was not only multiracial but
also multinational. On the night of the attack a large group
of Eastern Europeans were in the service. Some of them
died in the attack and others were injured. This international element added to the worldwide interest in the
event. But the most shocking thing of all was that this was
the first time in our troubled history that a church was
attacked in this way. Somehow an invisible line had been
crossed. A new level of depravity had been reached. If it

was intended as a political act of some sort, the act itself breached a most basic human right—the right to worship in peace and safety. It indicated a depth of psychopathic criminal thinking and behaviour that was too horrible to contemplate. Nothing was sacred any more. Nowhere was there either safety or respect. Unfortunately loss of respect appears endemic in our society as young and old are drawn into the political brutality of the day. It was in response to these things that we preached and taught and finally wrote.

There is nothing new in this book and certainly nothing that has not been said better elsewhere. But it does come out of the crucible of our own experience and I can only pray that it will strike a chord and be a help to others as they struggle with their own personal tragedies. I owe my staff and congregation a great deal of thanks for their prayers, love and support during these traumatic months. They have been a great encouragement to me as I have tried to capture the lessons we learned and put them on paper. Brian and Thy Cameron have helped to proofread the manuscript and have assisted me with many valuable suggestions. Heather, my secretary, has flying fingers. She has typed and retyped with great patience and much skill. My thanks go to Rhonda Crouse for her valuable editorial help. But I thank God especially for my wife Beulah and my children Grant, Bruce and Debby-Anne, for their patience with me during these past months. They seemed to sense that I was working through things for myself and that writing this book was my private therapy. I am so grateful to them. May God be pleased to use this book to bring hope and direction to others who are suffering, and glory to His own great name.

Frank J Retief

1

The St James Massacre

When the Boeing 747 touched down at DF Malan Airport in Cape Town on the morning of 25 July 1993, we all breathed a sigh of relief. It had been a long, cramped flight from London. We had enjoyed a wonderful holiday together as a family, a gift from a generous congregation after twenty-five years of ministry in the same church.

St James Church in Kenilworth started small. Four children made up the first 'congregation' when Beulah, my bride of nine months, and I arrived to take up our duties. Our mandate was to start a church in a part of the suburb that was designated for redevelopment. For reasons that still mystify us, we sensed the presence of God in our little church almost from the start.

The twenty-five years that have elapsed have seen the growth of that tiny group into a church campus that today houses various children's ministries, offices, a restaurant, a book shop, a library, meeting halls and an auditorium that seats 1500. Ten daughter churches have been established in a wide ring around the church. The eleventh 'daughter' is a community centre in the sprawling black township of Khayelitsha on the outskirts of Cape Town where hundreds of thousands of squatters have created a bustling city of tents, shacks and informal housing units. In the centre itself, scores of children found a shelter while their mothers are at work. Various self-help schemes have been initiated and church services, Sunday School classes and youth meetings are conducted, creating a kaleidoscope of activity and community interaction.

The little fellowship in Khayelitsha still carries the burden of the murderous attack on Chris Tebboth. Chris was a young volunteer from Sussex, England. As a committed Christian he felt he wanted to do something special with his life and thought of missionary services. At twenty-one his choices all still lay before him. He decided to test the waters by volunteering to work among youth in Africa. Through a chance meeting with my son Grant, who was in London at the time, Chris arrived in Cape Town and was soon happily immersed in the busy programme of the Khayelitsha Community Centre.

The Wednesday in Easter week saw Chris planning uneasily to spend the night in the community centre. The township is a volatile place. The complexities of South African politics have seen the rise of vast numbers of jobless township youth easily stirred up to march, demonstrate and riot. Nights in the township are often broken by the sound of gunfire. Chris went to sleep that night with a sense of foreboding.

The next morning he summoned the youth in the area to a vacant lot and arranged a soccer game. One teenager of seventeen had captured Chris's attention. He had tried to befriend the boy two days earlier and had met with some success. The game progressed and everyone seemed to enjoy it. Life around the vacant lot went on as usual. Suddenly the teenager drew a large calibre revolver from under his shirt and shot Chris in the back. Everyone froze. As Chris fell to the ground, the youth walked over to him and shot him twice more at point-blank range, one shot to the temple.

Mrs Noseseku, who runs the crèche at the community centre, heard the shots and ran outside to investigate.

She had a baby on her hip. She saw the teenager about to shoot again and screamed at him in horror. He turned, shot in her direction, and ran. Miraculously he missed her and, even more miraculously, Chris was still alive. There are no cars or telephones within easy access in that part of the township. At that very moment a social worker drew up in a motor car. Within minutes Chris was loaded into the car crying, 'Tell him I forgive him!'

The days that followed were filled with shock, tension, fear and confusion. Would Chris live? Why did the youth shoot him? The community in the township was outraged. Sympathy and love poured in from all over. We waited anxiously to hear whether Chris would make it or not. Three days later Chris Hani was assassinated.

Chris Hani was a charismatic and hugely popular figure in South African politics. He was the leader of the South African Communist Party and was involved in the sensitive negotiations for a new democratic political dispensation in South Africa. His assassination was a tragedy. I remember sitting in front of the television and weeping for our nation. Our country was being pushed to the brink of an abyss. For weeks we teetered on the edge of total chaos. Marches, demonstrations and immense anger swept the land, especially when white right-wing extremists were arrested for the crime.

The mood in Khayelitsha changed. Chris Tebboth and the tragedy that befell him were pushed to the background. Laura Haas and her team who head up the development in Khayelitsha could not go into the township. Chris himself lay suspended between life and death. The country was in chaos and a dark mood of pessimism swept the land. Christians across the nation prayed for peace and God's supernatural intervention.

Somehow the land and its people slowed down and caught its breath and a semblance of normality returned.

Chris rallied and began to recover. Eventually he was released from hospital. He had lost his sight in one eye but, by a strange twist of providence, his life had been spared. He returned home to England with clear instructions to seek help for post-traumatic stress. He had paid dearly for his experiment in Africa.

July 25 was a cold, wet winter's day in Cape Town. A month in an unseasonably humid London and a night in an aircraft had left us all longing for the bracing winter weather of Cape Town. Bruce and Debby-Anne had enjoyed the time with their elder brother Grant in London but now came the serious business of seeing friends, sharing the gifts they had purchased and regaling their peers with stories of their travels. Hugs and kisses over, we climbed into the car and set off for home. It was Sunday.

All my life I have been a poor traveller, so my headache from a sleepless night was nothing new. An afternoon nap did nothing to shake it. We were due to pack up and leave again for a seaside destination as soon as possible. I had reached a severe state of exhaustion prior to our holiday and had been only too glad to accept the two months leave insisted on by the church leaders. One month had passed and another month awaited us. There was therefore no rush to leave for our second destination so soon after landing. So, struggling with jet lag and not being expected back for another month, Beulah and I decided not to go to church that night. But Bruce and Debby-Anne just had to go. There were too many people they had not seen for a month. That night they went to a service that would change their lives forever.

St James Church has a reputation in Cape Town for a straightforward approach to the Bible and its message. Its no-nonsense services usually include singing popular choruses and hymns, a song item or two from gifted members of the congregation and a simple presentation of a

Bible passage. Over the years numbers of people have come to faith in Christ and often even non-members bring friends to the services to expose them to the claims of the Christian gospel.

One of the new developments in the life of the church has been its outreach programme to Eastern European seamen visiting the port. For years South Africans were taught to be suspicious of anything Russian. All Russians, we were led to believe, were 'the enemy' in some undefined way. Then the unthinkable happened. Communism began to crumble, the Berlin Wall was demolished, in South Africa Nelson Mandela was released from prison, and a new day dawned for South African politics. As a result the ships from Eastern Europe that plied trade in the South Atlantic Ocean began to visit our port again.

The catalyst for our church was a Russian scientific vessel that was trapped in the Antarctic. A rescue effort by South Africa saw a number of seamen stranded in Cape Town for several weeks.

Dawie and Marita Ackermann were deeply involved in the outreach activities at St James. Their Afrikaans background with its natural hospitality made them popular with everyone. Their comfortable home in Rondebosch was often thrown open for dinners and lunches with all kinds of people, lonely people, single people, new people who felt uncomfortable in church surroundings, hurting people. All found a welcome at the Ackermanns. Marita and Dawie immediately saw the evangelistic opportunity presented by a group of Russians far away from home, penniless and friendless.

Through a series of approaches, contact was made, hosts were arranged and the Russians were finally treated to a tour of the Cape Peninsula, a splendid supper at the church and a church service of which not one of them understood a word. The warmth and friendship of the Ackermanns and their team, the music and atmosphere of the church and the welcome they received made up for any shortfall in linguistics. Everyone got along happily with sign language, smiles and huge doses of bonhomie.

Slowly the ministry grew as other ships came to the port. We made contact with Alenora Paly, a Ukrainian emigrant who had settled in Cape Town with her husband and two children. Not only was she a trained translator, she was also a committed Christian.

A number of Russian ships had docked and contact was made with a large number of Eastern Europeans. Many of them had had no church contact in their entire lives. Others had just a passing brush with either the Orthodox Church or the Roman Catholic Church. There were 160 Russians in church on the night of July 25.

The congregation of about 1,300 on that blustery winter's evening was made up of people from all walks of life, both young and old. Many of those present have their own stories to tell of lives wasted by bad decisions and destructive habits, who have been reclaimed by the grace of God. Others were taking their first tentative steps towards the Christian faith. Some stubbornly refused to allow Christ to play any role whatever in their lives. The fact that such people come to church at all is one of the mysteries of the communal life at St James, yet they come to listen to God's Word with its presentation of a Saviour and its offer of a salvation so different form the tawdry offerings of the world they inhabit.

The music at St James has always been an important part of the services. As the years have passed, many gifted and talented people have come into the church. An attempt has been made to make room for them so that their gifts may be used to the glory of God. As part of the programme that Sunday night, Tanya and Neil sang a duet called 'More Than Wonderful'.

Over the years different political groups in South Africa have adopted a philosophy of violence as a means of overthrowing the apartheid government. However, with the new approach led by President F W de Klerk and the start of political negotiations for a democratic future, most parties have, for the time being anyway, laid down their arms. But not all have done so. There are some who engage in provocative war talk and have threatened to attack soft targets. In fact certain soft targets had been hit: a country club, a number of restaurants and various government buildings have been bombed. Farmers in isolated areas have been murdered. It has slowly become evident that often the attackers are not controlled by their high commands. Illegal supplies of guns proliferate in South Africa . Unemployed youths armed with automatic weapons stalk the townships. Crime has increased dramatically and often the perpetrators claim a political affiliation in the hope that their crimes will be seen as political acts. Despite this climate of violence, nobody ever expected an attack on people at worship. It was unthinkable in a country where two-thirds of the population claim some form of Christian affiliation.

The door next to the stage opened as the duet was ending. The congregation sat listening to the sweet strains of the song slowly dying. Then the gunmen burst in. A man in dark clothing stood there with an R4 automatic weapon in his hand.

The audience gazed at him with innocent curiosity. Strangers often come into the church, but this one was unusually late. No one realised the significance of his action when he awkwardly swung his rifle from one hand to the other, indicating that he was left-handed. Then he opened fire.

A number of people thought it was all staged. St James has from time to time used drama as a means of communicating or illustrating the gospel message. People thought this was another such occasion. A woman sitting in the wing of the church was annoyed. She had spent all morning in mission work outside the church. This was the one service she was able to attend on a Sunday, and she relished it. Why, she thought to herself, are people letting off fireworks in church?

We have had irate neighbours complain about the bad parking habits of some of our congregants. They have from time to time threatened drastic damage to the vehicles and in fact once a car's tyres were deflated. But surely they would not go this far?

The bullets raked the congregation. Curiosity gave way to shock and terror. Marita Ackermann sat in her usual place in the front pew with Alenora Paly and the contingent from the ships. Her husband Dawie had moved off at the last minute to sit next to a Russian visitor who was on his own. Marita was hit while Alenora was unscathed. As injured people began to scream and the congregation tried to take cover, the gunmen lobbed a hand grenade attached to a tin of nails into the audience. The explosion wrecked pews and blew hundreds of pieces of deadly shrapnel in all directions. Gerhard and Wesley Harker were in church for the second successive Sunday. Spiritually, something was beginning to awaken in them. New horizons were opening for them. As the grenade landed, something happened. Some said that Gerhard threw himself on the grenade to protect his brother. If so, it was a tragically futile action. Both boys died.

Richard Okill was a clergyman's son. His parents had returned to England to start a new life there leaving Richard behind to finish his final year of schooling. Richard was a boisterous, likeable young man. As many others do, he had gone through a time of spiritual uncertainty and doubt, but in recent months had seemed to find his direction. He sat with two friends, Bonnie and Lisa. In an instinctive act of courage, he threw himself over the two girls and was shot in the back.

Denise Gordon, mother of three-year-old Sarah, was killed instantly. Sarah was in the foyer with her grandmother, Era, who runs the restaurant. Denise's husband Peter was badly injured.

Myrtle Smith was hit and died on the floor of the church.

Guy Javens died on the floor next to his wife, Marilynn.

Marita Ackermann died on her way to hospital.

Five of the Eastern European visitors were killed on their first night in a Christian church.

Fifty-three people were listed as wounded, some seriously. Hospitals and rescue services were swamped.

Still trying to shake my headache, I decided to open some of the mail that had accumulated while we were away when the doorbell rang. Lynda is an old family friend. She had recently been instrumental in starting a prayer meeting for Jewish evangelism. In a state of shock, she blurted out what had happened at the church. The horror of the picture she painted was so great that I struggled to grasp it. I rushed to the church immediately.

It seemed as though a million lights were flashing as I walked past ambulances, police vehicles and rescue services in stunned amazement. People were talking in small groups. Already the media had gathered.

I could not believe what I saw inside the building. Bodies draped with sheets were lying in the aisles. In the upper rows of pews, paramedics were desperately trying to pump Myrtle Smith's heart. In a daze, I heard her husband Lorenzo say to me, 'They don't think she'll make it!'

She didn't.

Pews were splintered and a makeshift stretcher had

been formed. People were trying to lift Dimitri, one of the Russians, onto it. One of the church members trying to help looked up at me with anguish and whispered, 'This man has no legs.'

He had lost both legs and an arm.

Where are my children, I thought to myself. Fear gripped my heart. I stopped someone and asked, 'Have you seen Bruce and Debby-Anne?'

'No,' they replied, 'but many people had been taken away by ambulance.'

Then I saw Marilynn Javens in Laura Haas's arms. I sat next to them in shock.

'Guy is dead,' Laura informed me.

Where are my children, I wondered as horror gripped me. There was blood everywhere—on pews, carpets, clothing. I stopped someone and asked them to phone my home and find out if the children were there. Slowly the names of those who had been killed or injured were passed to me. About twenty minutes later someone told me that my children were safe at home. Bruce had helped put bodies onto stretchers then taken his sister home. She was badly shocked. I was immensely relieved to know that they were safe but unspeakably sad as I thought of those who would never make it home.

Numbers of people came onto the church premises. Neighbours came to see if they could help. Relatives who knew their family members were in the service came to look for them. Ministers of churches in the area came to see if they could help. The media were interviewing members and witnesses all over the campus. Dawie Ackermann and his children were filmed appearing calm and unshaken as they offered forgiveness to the men who had killed Marita. The media were unable to detect hurt or shock in the reaction of the family. Microphones were pushed under my nose, questions were fired at me and the full glare of media attention descended on our church.

The next two weeks passed as a blurred memory, a collage of interviews, questions, police, telephones, faxes and telegrams. Local supermarkets supplied sandwiches and soup as the police set up a command post on the premises and hundreds of people bustled around. Suddenly decisions had to be made on the spur of the moment about radio and TV programmes, interviews with the press, funeral arrangements, pastoral care and meeting the dignitaries who arrived at the scene.

In a totally unexpected way, all we believed as Christians was thrown into sharp relief. How do you explain this? Why do you react as you do? Why did your people not panic? Why do they appear so calm? Why do you offer forgiveness? Where was God when this happened? The gospel in which we had put our trust was on the line.

A strange and unusual calm descended on me after the first shock passed. It is difficult to articulate this to those who have never been in a similar situation but many will know the reality of the experience of the presence of the One who is 'a very present help in trouble' (Psalm 46:1). He became 'very present' that night and in the days that followed.

After all the injured had been taken to hospital and all the bereaved had been gently entrusted to family and friends, I called aside all our staff members and leaders who were present for a quick emergency planning session. We would need to implement an organisational plan of some sort for the coming days.

First we decided who would do what. We set up a press conference for the following morning so that we could cover as many of the media as possible in one session. I worked till the early hours of the morning on a press statement which was checked and corrected by various men in our leadership. It was agreed that I would be the one to handle the press.

Next we had to provide pastoral care for the bereaved and the injured. We placed this responsibility in the hands of Barry van Eyssen and Ross Anderson. They kept in touch personally with the worst cases. We set up teams to monitor individual families and to update us on their progress and needs. Meals were provided for these families and they were cared for in every way possible. The monitors reported to Barry and Ross.

Then we had to establish debriefing sessions. The effects of post-traumatic stress cannot be overemphasised. Everyone reacts differently to trauma, but everyone needs to be debriefed. We asked Dr Angelo Grazioli to set this up. We used police psychiatrists while our own counsellors added the spiritual dimension. We urged everyone who was in church that night to attend the sessions and invited their relatives to join them. We went further and invited the people in the neighbourhood who had also been traumatised by the massacre. We realised that the children would need special treatment so separate sessions were arranged for children, teenagers and adults. Some people needed more in-depth personal counselling than the group debriefing sessions permitted. This was arranged.

We established a team of legal and financial experts to assist us with the setting up of a relief fund drawing on our denominational personnel for this. They drew up the necessary documentation and assisted us in briefing the press about this matter.

A difficult task facing us was to get people to return to the building. It was a major psychological barrier to overcome. Many people came back to the scene of the atrocity of their own accord but others had to be encouraged to do so. They came with family and friends to show them where they had sat, then collapsed into their arms in tears. We urged as many as possible to return and sit in the same seats and face the reality of what had happened.

A separate team was asked to plan the funerals. Special services had to be arranged and brochures had to be produced at short notice. We left this in the hands of a gifted graphic artist who understood what we wanted. The bereaved had to be consulted sensitively about the funerals which had to be planned carefully because of media interest. We needed special grace in all our public utterances because of the political overtones that hung threateningly in the air.

And then we had to face our own public meetings and church services. The congregation needed direction. They needed to know that we were not floundering. Following the suggestion of a friend, I announced a series of sermons entitled 'The Road to Recovery'. Immediately we all knew where we were going.

People filled the buildings the first Sunday after the event. Many of them were strangers we had never seen before who felt traumatised and wanted help. There were numerous unspoken questions. Difficult issues had to be articulated and an honest attempt made to answer them with integrity.

The attack on our church did not last more than thirty seconds, but it was thirty seconds that shook the nation, brought worldwide condemnation of political violence and changed the lives of literally thousands of people forever. It made us face the deep questions of life. It forced us to confront the mysteries of our existence in this world the fearsome reality of evil and the massive display of goodwill and sympathy. It forced us to reflect on our view of God and his relationship to good and evil, and it forced us to look the world in the face and answer for the things we believe.

Tragedy and its aftermath

It is not possible to capture all the drama, events and emotions of that time in a few short pages, but I have recounted the main events of the St James massacre for two reasons. Firstly, the massacre received universal news coverage because of the nature of the attack and the international ramifications of foreigners being murdered by terrorists. Secondly, the aftermath of this tragedy is in essence no different from the aftermath of any other tragedy.

Suffering, as we all know, is part of our experience in this life. It has occasioned many questions and many books have been written on the subject. Tragedy adds an edge to the experience of suffering. It brings an additional element of sadness and unhappiness to the sufferer. All tragedy involves suffering but not all suffering is a tragedy in the commonly accepted understanding of the term. For instance, an elderly person of ninety-five who has lost sight and hearing and sinks into a slow illness that leads to death may rightly be said to suffer. But we expect elderly people to die eventually because this is the way of all flesh. On the other hand, the death of the young parents of three small children in a freak accident brings an added element of sadness to the suffering because small children need their parents and are likely to suffer more greatly without them.

Tragedy may take many forms. A young girl who lives promiscuously and indulges in drink, drugs and dangerous company may well bring great suffering on herself. But an innocent teenager whose home is broken into and who is raped by an unknown assailant can be said to have suffered a tragedy.

It is hard to define tragedy too closely because suffering takes on different meanings for different people. But when the unexpected happens and loss of life, limb or love is experienced; when lives are turned upside down; when great universally held moral codes are deliberately defied and the common sense of justice and fairness is violated, a tragedy has occurred. When something needless, pointless, cruel, vindictive and malicious robs us of our values, sense of well-being, security or respect, we stand face to face with tragedy.

Your own personal tragedy is probably very different to what we experienced in our church. You may have your own tale of sadness and overwhelming grief. To each person the events in their lives that bring sorrow and tears carry their own significance. Proverbs 14: 10 says: 'Each heart knows its own bitterness.' The cup from which we are sometimes called to drink may be bitter. Divorce, abuse, misplaced trust, victims of crime, accidents, sickness, war, death. Whatever it may be, we all have to find a way to explain what has happened to us and to integrate what we have experienced into our world view.

How do we do this? How do we answer the questions that suffering and tragedy raise? No one is exempt from the uncertainties that plague us in this world, not even Christians who have a unique relationship with God through Jesus Christ. Christians suffer too. How then should we respond to suffering and tragedy? Do we simply say it is the devil? Do we try to exonerate God from responsibility? Or do we blame ourselves and say it was because we had no faith or too little faith? What do Christians say when they are plunged to the depths of horror and human experience overwhelms them with sorrow? Is it ever right for a Christian to enter into the dismal experience of the Psalmist who said:

I say to God my Rock
'Why have you forgotten me?

2

Why Me, Lord?

It became very clear to the nation and to the world on the dreadful night of July 25 that Christians do indeed suffer and that at they are sometimes called to suffer terribly. The confusion this caused was expressed by a number of people who value the Bible-centred ministry of St James. 'But why St James?' they cried. If a church was going to be attacked, why not a church that was not committed to the gospel, whose presence and ministry was irrelevant? Why choose a church with such a well-known commitment not only to the gospel but also to the community? More clear-sighted people simply wanted to know why Christians have to experience this kind of suffering at all.

The single factor that probably needs to be addressed more than any other is the belief that Christians who experience suffering should have sufferings that are reasonable. It is one thing for us to read books about martyrs and those who are persecuted in faraway lands. We are all encouraged by stories of great heroism and bravery in the face of death. It is quite another, in our Western society, to be called on suddenly to experience trauma of this nature.

There is an unspoken feeling among Christians that, if there is to be suffering, it should be bearable and that we should not experience the same horror that unbelievers do. The truth of the matter is that we are often exposed to the same depth of suffering. Our sufferings are not always reasonable. In fact, they sometimes appear to be more than we can bear. Grief and sorrow overwhelm us and we feel as though we are sinking. This is a plain fact of human experience in this world. But should it be this way? Does God not support his people when they experience tragedy? Are his promises meaningless or is there substance to them after all? Does God not promise to protect his people?

There are many great Scripture statements the believer may cling to, but for many Christians the truth is that poor Scripture instruction causes them to come to wrong conclusions. For instance, the promises of protection in Scripture often refer to God's power to keep his people faithful to him. God promises to protect his people from falling away into apostasy. He promises to keep us safe in a state of salvation until our salvation is consummated in heaven. It would be wonderful if the gospel promises included freedom from sickness, disease and poverty, and deliverance from danger and adversity. Instead Scripture teaches us that part of God's discipling process in our lives is to leave us in this fallen world to cope with opposition and danger so that our faith may be tested and we may learn to be holy.

This does not mean that there are never occasions when God rescues his people miraculously. Nor does it mean to suggest that God never hears our prayers, never heals us, never guides, protects or provides for us. On the contrary, the story of the church of Jesus Christ is full of testimonies of supernatural intervention, sometimes at the most crucial moment. But we must balance these glorious possibilities against the simple fact that God does not remove us from a world of trouble and suffering the moment we put our trust in Christ.

Reactions to suffering

We all react differently to suffering and tragedy but

15

there are certain common denominators we all face in times of great trauma. I want to refer to these briefly, but first I want to highlight two hazards Christians face after a time of great suffering.

The first is an exaggerated sense of heroism, persecution or destiny. They enjoy a certain peace. They have an awareness of the presence of the Lord and therefore feel that they are above the common disturbances and heartaches of life. They seem to run on adrenaline for a while and appear to have amazing inner peace to the mystification of all around them.

It must be stressed that many Christians in traumatic situations do experience the presence of God in a very real way. Many people would give eloquent testimony to this fact. If you have experienced some form of tragedy, you are most likely also able to testify that God drew near to you in a special way. However, if your reactions are not rooted in a firm biblical foundation, if you are not realistic about what has happened to you, if you allow yourself to be carried along on adrenaline alone, you may be headed for a crash.

Often during those heady moments after a disaster, when attention is focused on the believer, there is a feeling of such spiritual strength that debriefing and counselling are not desired. This is a dangerous time that calls for discernment. A distinction must be made between the gracious power of God who does indeed draw near to his children in days of trauma to protect them, and the fact that we are human and are not exempt from the normal emotional responses that others experience. If we are not careful, we may enter a time of depression and anticlimax when the spotlight is switched off and the adrenaline has stopped pumping. Confused and bewildered, we could find ourselves experiencing exactly the same problems others had but which we were able to suppress for a while.

The second danger is false guilt. Some Christians do experience the symptoms of stress from the outset but feel that they should not be subject to stress factors because they are Christians. They feel that to admit their need for help would be to deny the reality of God in their lives. To need help means that they are failing spiritually. They have erroneously concluded that true Christian spirituality is to be unaffected by the pain of living in this fallen world. Nothing could be further from the truth. If our Lord and Saviour Himself shed tears while He was on earth, why shouldn't we?

It may be helpful to describe some of the common reactions to extreme suffering in a little more detail. The following description of tragedy is taken from an investigation by the American Psychiatric Association published in a report entitled 'Diagnostic and Statistical Manual of Mental Disorders'. Bear in mind that we are dealing here with tragedy rather than suffering.

> The most common traumata involve either a serious threat to one's life or physical integrity; a serious threat or harm to one's children, spouse, or other close relatives and friends; sudden destruction of one's home or community, or seeing another person who has recently been, or is being, seriously injured or killed as the result of an accident or physical violence. In some cases the trauma may be learning about a serious threat or harm to a close friend or relative, e.g., that one's child has been kidnapped, tortured, or killed.
>
> The trauma may be experienced alone (e.g., rape or assault) or in the company of groups of people (e.g., military combat). Stressors producing this disorder include natural disasters

(e.g., floods, earthquakes), accidental disasters
(e.g., car accidents with serious physical injury,
aeroplane crashes, large fires, collapse of physical structures), or deliberately caused disasters
(e.g., bombing, torture, death camps).

Although much of this is not the sort of thing we
are likely to experience, for example military combat, earthquakes, aeroplane crashes, many do experience physical
threats, rapes, accidents and violence. The kind of suffering described here lies above the norm and outside the
range of usual human experiences. But it happens in our
world today and even believing Christians may be caught
up in it. It is important for us to be aware of the consequences of this kind of trauma. Again this has been helpfully summarised in the American Psychiatric Association
report. Speaking about the horror of re-experiencing the
event, the report points out that reactions to extreme suffering can include the following:

- Disturbing recollections of the event.
- Distressing dreams.
- Psychological distress at anything that reminds them of the event.
- Avoiding anything that will trigger memory.
- A general psychic numbing or emotional
  anaesthesia, i.e. an inability to feel or respond. This is expressed by a loss of enjoyment of life, loss of ability to feel or
  respond to any kind of intimacy or tenderness.

In our experience at St James, we saw many of these
symptoms manifested. It took some people a while before
they felt emotionally strong enough to go back to the

church premises. Others were plagued by nightmares, dreams and horrific thoughts. Many people slept with their lights on. Everyone felt jittery. Many were startled by any loud noise, however innocent the source. In your own personal tragedy, you may experience a number of these reactions to a varying extent.

We also need to remember that some people who experience a sadness or tragedy may have had deep-rooted problems before the tragedy struck. The symptoms of the former emotional problem may for a while be confused with the reactions to the later event. I will refer to this again in Chapter 5. I merely want to draw attention to this possibility at this point.

One of the major problems facing many of our people after the massacre was irritability. This was accompanied by a loss of concentration and difficulty falling or staying asleep. This in turn was accompanied by increased aggression. All these things added to the struggles these people faced in coming to terms with their emotions while trying to maintain a clear Christian witness to their family and community.

In dealing with reactions to suffering and tragedy, we need to remember that children display specific symptoms. Once again the American Psychiatric Association report provides helpful guidelines for dealing with traumatised children.

> Occasionally, a child may be mute or refuse to discuss the trauma, but this should not be confused with inability to remember what occurred. In younger children, distressing dreams of the event may, within several weeks, change into generalized nightmares of monsters, of rescuing others, or of threats to self or others. Young children do not have the sense that they are reliving the past; reliving the trauma oc-

curs in action, through repetitive play.

Diminished interest in significant activities and constriction of affect both may be difficult for children to report on themselves, and should be carefully evaluated by reports from parents, teachers, and other observers. A symptom of Post-traumatic Stress Disorder in children may be a marked change in orientation toward the future. This includes the sense of foreshortened future, for example, a child may not expect to have a career or marriage. There may also be 'omen formation', that is, belief in an ability to prophesy future untoward events.

Children may exhibit various physical symptoms, such as stomachaches and headaches, in addition to the specific symptoms of increased arousal noted above.

After the events in our church, we asked the children in our Sunday School to write letters to God. This was part of the debriefing process in helping the children to come to terms with what had happened. One child wrote the following:

Dear God

Even though they tell us to not be afraid I'm still very scared. I don't know what will become of South Africa until the elections. I think Sunday night was terrible I'm very, very, very, very scared.

Love

P.S. I heard about the church on T.V.

If you have been through a major marital upheaval,
an accident or a loss of some kind, remember that as Christians we live in an imperfect world. It is a world dominated by sin and selfishness, a world that is alienated from
God. The judgement of God on this world and the upheavals we experience in society do not leave the children
of God unscathed. If you have been exposed to teaching
that has led you to believe that Christians should be specially protected from sorrows of this nature, you may be
constantly confused by the events that happen around you.
I urge you to be aware of the world in which we live and
to understand that the Scriptures do not promise us a life
free of trial and tribulation. On the contrary, Christians
are warned to expect trouble in this world. Be realistic
about life and your walk with God.

Coping with suffering

For Christians who have been through serious trauma,
it is very important to seek expert counselling help. In
our own case we organised two weeks of debriefing sessions for adults and children. We all needed help and, in
God's goodness, the right people were on hand to help
us. We were assisted by a team of psychiatrists from the
Police Department. They were sensitive enough to understand that, having identified the stress disorders and
offered some suggestions, they could not proceed into
the realm of biblical teaching and response. They therefore worked alongside our own church counselling teams
who were able to add the spiritual dimension and to place
the debriefing process in a biblical framework. At the
same time two hard questions were answered. Yes, Christians can be called to suffer in this way, and yes, even Christians need help in a crisis.

If you have faced a serious trauma, you may need someone to help you in a similar way. Often people who are not actually involved in the tragedy are close enough to be traumatised. Their trauma is prolonged because of the overwhelming sense of sadness that grips them.

Once again, Christians face two dangers. The one is to seek purely spiritual advice from untrained people who are unable to deal with and explain some of the natural responses we have to tragedy. Often these well-meaning people simply pray or rebuke the devil. This kind of superficial response only complicates the situation because the stress disorders are not identified and dealt with. On the other hand, Christians sometimes place themselves in the hands of professional counsellors, psychiatrists or psychologists who are expert at identifying the disorder but do not have the expertise to help the believer to integrate the experience into their Christian faith. Christians therefore need to seek the help of professional people with appropriate training who are also sensible biblical counsellors, people who will help them to deal realistically and biblically with their feelings.

A word of caution is necessary. We need to remember that dealing successfully with our feelings is not something that happens overnight. One or two sessions of biblical counselling will not necessarily put everything back into place, but by placing yourself under the ministry of the Word of God, you will learn proper Christian responses.

A debriefing or a counselling period is extremely valuable. It focuses on the inner struggles you are going through as a result of a time of great pain for you. While your belief and faith in God may remain firm, you nevertheless enter a new struggle in your relationship with him.

In our case, several factors contributed to the sense of shock in the congregation. First there was the feeling that a crime of this nature should not have happened in the church. It seemed as if an invisible line had been crossed and the forces of evil had taken on new dimensions. One child in our Sunday School wrote:

> Dear God,
>
> Why did it have to happen to us.
> I mean if you're not safe in a church where
> are you safe. I feel nervous about coming to
> Sunday School and I feel nervous about talk-
> ing about it.

She expressed exactly what many people around the nation and in fact around the world felt about the massacre. Violence has reached a level of extreme revulsion when a soft target such as a church is attacked. You may feel in your own personal circumstance that whatever happened should not have happened to you or your family. A sense of moral outrage grips you if a violation has taken place such as the rape of an innocent young girl or the death of a good person in a hit-and-run accident. We felt the same way, the setting and the circumstances were all wrong for a crime of this nature.

A second problem we faced was the horrible way in which people died. In the explosive world of South African politics, violence has become a part of the everyday experience of many people. Horror story after horror story erupts on the front pages of our newspapers as bombs and bullets take their deadly toll. But what happens in the sprawling townships of our land now suddenly came home to us with great force. Maimed and injured people lay before us. Blood congealed thickly on our pews. Corpses lay in the aisles. The days that followed were filled with stories of broken bones, horrific injuries, skin grafts, crutches and wheelchairs. The horror of the situation gripped our minds and was expressed by the reluctance of some people to come back into the building. This was the first great barrier that many had to cross.

In your experience, the way in which your tragedy occurred may be stark in your mind. The way in which you were deceived by a loved one, the freak nature of an accident that took away a family member or the blatancy of a crime that disrupted your life leads to a sense of horror and insecurity.

A third factor that had an impact on us as a congregation was the pathos of the situation. Here were a group of people who represented a cross section of our society. They came to church with their heartaches, longings, aspirations, hopes and fears. Some had recently become Christians and were beginning to find their way spiritually. Others, like the Russians and Eastern Europeans, had never been in church before and were filled with curiosity and interest. Some were elderly, some were young. Suddenly what was meant to be a time of joy, worship and fellowship was turned into a night of grief. Mothers, fathers and children all gone in a matter of seconds. The impact of this situation was enormous, and so it may be with you too.

In our case it was all so futile and unnecessary. In the peculiar political context of this country, points are scored by hitting soft targets, but this horrific crime scored points for nobody. There was such an international outcry that no political party accepted responsibility for the act. In fact it has become evident that the perpetrators were probably a cadre of terrorists who made an error in judgement. They did not expect such a universal condemnation of their deed.

Called to suffer

This brings us back to the problem of the believer in Christ and the depth of suffering he may be called to endure. Paul lists his sufferings in 2 Corinthians 11:16–33.

He mentions that his hardships included not only persecution from the authorities but also dangers from other causes: shipwrecks, drowning in rivers, bandits, hunger, sleeplessness, labour and toil. In other words, as an apostle he was not exempt from the normal run of daily hardships in addition to his struggles as a messenger of Christ. Even Christians are subject to the dangers and struggles of living in a world that is imperfect and alienated from God.

The word we give to this condition is 'fallen'. We are a people who have fallen from our state of innocence and fellowship with our Creator. Our sin has caused us to 'fall'. When we fell, the world fell too, so that we live as fallen people in a fallen world. Our 'fallenness' is seen in our society with its war and crime; its inability to accomplish true justice and peace; its racism and bigotry; its hatred and intolerance, and its quick resort to war and weapons of destruction. But our fallenness is seen too in the sickness, diseases, plagues and frailties that beset the human race. Our very bodies carry within them the sentence of death. The fallenness of our world is seen further in the great tumults of natural disasters: earthquakes, famines, floods and storms. It is almost as if the whole of creation occasionally heaves a sigh of frustration and when it does so, man is seen once again to be the small, puny creature that he is; not, after all, the master of his own destiny.

In all these things the people of God suffer as well. Floods, hurricanes, earthquakes, war, disease affect us all. Faith in Christ protects us from hopelessness and despair but does not prevent the storm from breaking. Like the rest of the human race, we have to seek for refuge and help. In addition to this, Christians sometimes face the added difficulty of persecution and discrimination because of their faith. For most Christians in the Western world, persecution may take fairly mild forms. But in many parts of our world it can take a vicious turn and result in torture, imprisonment and death.

Even in the present mood of tolerance that calls for the acceptance of religious pluralism, Christians face a new danger. As this pluralism becomes the 'politically correct' stance, it may give rise to a situation where the exclusivism of our faith is outlawed as primitivism and bigotry.

No, dear friends, it is not a safe world. We may choose to be deluded and try to build our little havens, but the world with its uncertainties will find a way in. If we refuse to recognise this and insist on our rights to special protection, we will soon be disillusioned. This is why so many Christian counsellors are kept busy with people who can be described as dropouts from the prosperity cults. They were taught a theology that saw no place for suffering, but it did not work in their experience. Hurt and confused, they need to be guided back to the bedrock of God's Word.

The truth is that Christians really do suffer and are sometimes called to suffer terribly. The further truth is that even the best of God's children often stand in need of help when life hurls its worst at them. But this raises another question, should it? If God loves His people, should there not be some special protection for them? Do His promises mean anything? Is He really all-powerful? Have Christians in some mysterious way been fooled all along? When the chips are down, is He really there for us? In other words, can God really be trusted?

3

Can God be Trusted?

One of the things that puzzled the media in the aftermath of the St James massacre was the attitude of the people. In fact it was not only the media who were puzzled. The rescue services commented on the orderly and controlled way the congregation behaved in vacating the building and the absence of hysteria. Some of the Christians in the building testified to an overwhelming sense of peace and conviction of God's overriding control even while the shooting was taking place.

Then came the professions of forgiveness. The international media found this hard to cope with and frequently questioned me about it . The truth is that I did not even know what people were saying to the media until days afterwards. I can say in all honesty that while I encountered shock, horror, grief, sadness and anger, I have not come across anyone who felt embittered towards God. There was very little questioning of God by the people involved.

But the outside world had a field day. People phoned radio stations and flooded newspapers with letters demanding answers to their questions. Where was God? What did these Christians have to say now? How did they explain this? And so on. It is also true that many professing Christians from other churches and organisations had a lot to say. St James provided topics for sermons and magazine articles for weeks—some of these bordering on the blasphemous.

There were certainly questions in the minds of many of the Christians in our church, but they were not the questions born out of lack of trust. Rather, they were questions born of grief and confusion. It appeared that the years of systematic Bible study had borne fruit in a time of great darkness. But naturally questions did arise. One Sunday School child tried valiantly to express his feelings and his theology in the following letter:

> Dear God
>
> Please help all the people who were in the church at the time that the incident happened. Lord, I am also confused because I don't know why you let them [the terrorists] do it, but Lord as you say in the book of Job When we ask our why questions you may not answer it straight away but you are always in control.

You may have the same struggle in your own life. When a partner whom we have loved and trusted proves unfaithful, our whole world goes into a tailspin. Feelings of panic and disaster overwhelm us. If some area of our life has been dreadfully violated by crime or tragedy, the instinctive reaction is to seek a reason. We automatically assume that an effect must have a cause. And if we can isolate the cause, we can at least understand why that thing happened. It is something tangible to hold onto, and the element of mystery is banished.

Most of us have both sets of feelings whirling around inside us. On the one hand there is a genuine trust in God. We love him and resolutely refuse to believe that He has abandoned us. On the other hand we are engulfed by a sense of grief and loss and feel the need of some explanations.

A complicating factor for believers facing tragedy is that they need to give some answer to the watching world. It is non-believers who are most vociferous in demanding some explanation from God. They get angry, become outraged and strident in their demand for God to be just and fair. Justice and fairness to them, in situations like these, means that bad things should happen primarily to bad people. Good people who are devout and ethical in their lifestyles should be left untouched by human suffering. Often Christians have to face a world angered by unexplained tragedy while they are battling to come to terms with what has happened. They are still integrating the experience into their view of God and their relationship with him. The world rages, 'If God is a God of love, why did he let this happen?' While the trusting Christian whispers, 'My bones suffer mortal agony as my foes taunt me, saying to me all day long, Where is your God?' (Psalm 42:10).

We will deal with the question of why it happened in Chapter four. The question we need to deal with first is: Can God be trusted? Is he really a refuge in times of trouble? Let us consider the words of Psalm 91:9–12:

> If you make the Most High your dwelling
> even the Lord, who is my refuge
> then no harm will befall you,
> no disaster will come near your tent.
> For He will command His angels
>   concerning you
> to guard you in all your ways;
> they will lift you up in their hands,
> so that you will not strike your foot
> against a stone.

Are these promises true? Can God really be trusted or

have we all made a monumental mistake? Is it all just a nice idea that does not wash in the real world of bombs and bullets, crime and accidents, earthquakes and famine? In other words, before we can get to the 'why', we need to face the primary question of the character of God.

The answer from a Christian perspective is, quite obviously, that God can be trusted. But our trust in him will be greatly enhanced if we understand his relationship to good and evil. Let us look first at the quality of faithfulness.

Faithfulness

Unfaithfulness is one of the most prominent sins of our age. In the business world, the social world, the marriage bond, the home and even in the church world, we are far more accustomed to people not keeping their word than vice versa. Our society is littered with broken promises, ruined dreams, unmet expectations, cynicism and destructive suspicion. Faithfulness is a quality not generally expected in our world.

The reason for this is that to be faithful to each other, we have to be other-person-centred. This means that we must so value the other person that their interests and well-being are our primary concern. The truth is that by nature we are selfish and self-centred. Our own happiness usually comes first. Truthfulness, loyalty and commitment are not high on our personal agendas.

Against this background of disappointment in our daily experience, the Bible announces God to be faithful. We are invited to lift our eyes above the world we live in to the One who is faithful in all things, to all people, at all times. He is faithful to us because he is true to His own nature. Over and over again the word 'faithful' is used to described God's character and attributes. Consider the following Scriptures:

Know therefore that the Lord your God is God;
He is the faithful God, keeping His covenant
of love to a thousand generations of those who
love Him and keep His commands.

> (Deuteronomy 7:9)

Your love, O Lord, reaches to the heavens,
your faithfulness to the skies.

> (Psalm 36:5)

Spurgeon says about this verse:

Far, far above all comprehension is the truth
and faithfulness of God. He never fails, never
forgets, never falters, nor forfeits his Word.
Afflictions are like clouds, but the divine
truthfulness is all around them. While we are
under the cloud we are in the region of God's
faithfulness; when we move above it we shall
not need such an assurance. To every word
of threat a promise, prophecy or covenant,
the Lord has exactly adhered, for He is not a
man that He should lie, nor the Son of Man
that He should repent. (Treasury of David,
volume 2, p. 176)

In Psalm 89:8 we read:

O Lord God Almighty, who is like you?
You are mighty, O Lord, and your
faithfulness surrounds you.

Again let Spurgeon instruct us.

Men often fail in truth because their power

is limited and they find it easier to break their
word than to keep it; but the strong Jehovah
is equal to all His engagements, and will assuredly keep them. Unrivalled might and un-
paralleled truth are wedded in the character
of Jehovah. Blessed be His name that it is so.
(Ibid, volume 4, p. 158)

God's faithfulness is seen not only in His actions on
behalf of His people, but also in his actions in judgment
against those who oppose Him. His faithfulness is seen in
the way He is true to his character. To illustrate this aspect of God's faithfulness, let us look at what the apostle
Paul says:

If we disown Him,
He will also disown us;
if we are faithless,
He will remain faithful,
for He cannot disown himself.
(2 Timothy 2:12–13)

John Stott explains these verses as follows:

This other pair of epigrams envisages the
dreadful possibility of our denying Christ and
proving faithless. The first phrase 'if we deny
Him, He also will deny us' seems to be an
echo of our Lord's own warning: 'whoever
denies me before men, I also will deny before my Father who is in heaven'
(Matthew 10:33).

What then of the second phrase 'if we are
faithless, He remains faithful'? It has often

been taken as a comforting assurance that, even if we turn away from Christ, He will not turn away from us, for He will never be faithless as we are. And it is true, of course, that God never exhibits the fickleness or the faithlessness of man. Yet the logic of the Christian hymn, with its two pairs of balancing epigrams, really demands a different interpretation. 'If we deny Him' and 'if we are faithless' are parallels, which requires that 'He will deny us' and 'He remains faithful' be parallels also. In this case His 'faithfulness' when we are faithless will be faithfulness to His warnings. As William Hendriksen puts it: 'Faithfulness on his part means carrying out His threats ... as well as His promises.' So He will deny us, as the earlier epigram asserts. Indeed, if He did not deny us (in faithfulness to His plain warnings), He would then deny himself. But one thing is certain about God beyond any doubt or uncertainty whatever, and that is 'He cannot deny himself'. (The Message of 2 Timothy, p. 64)

The quality of faithfulness is essential to God's being. If He were not faithful, He would not be God. To be unfaithful or untrustworthy is to act contrary to his nature. This is of course impossible. We remind ourselves again of Spurgeon's words: 'He never fails, never forgets, never falters, nor forfeits His Word.'

God is not a man, that He should lie,
nor a son of man, that He should
change his mind.
Does He speak and then not act?

Does He promise and not fulfil?

(Numbers 23:19)

But if all this is true, how do we explain the tragedies of life? How does the event that happened in my life and yours tie up with His promise to love, keep, provide and protect? If He was able to stop it, but didn't, what are we to make of it?

God and the problem of good and evil

The problem of God's relationship to good and evil has been present for a long time. One of the psalmists of Israel wrestled with this problem long before Christ was born. Writing about the arrogance and the prosperity of wicked people, he shares his inner struggle:

> They have no struggles;
> their bodies are healthy and strong.
> They are free from the burdens common to
> man;
> they are not plagued by human ills.
> Therefore pride is their necklace;
> they clothe themselves with violence.
> From their callous hearts comes iniquity;
> the evil conceits of their minds know no
> limits.
> They scoff, and speak with malice;
> in their arrogance they threaten oppression.
> Their mouths lay claim to heaven,
> and their tongues take possession of the earth.
> Therefore their people turn to them
> and drink up waters in abundance.
> They say, 'How can God know?

Does the Most High have knowledge?'
This is what the wicked are like
always carefree, they increase in wealth.

(Psalm 73:4–12)

The conceit, malice and violence of wicked people
seems to go unchecked. Instead of suffering some form
of judgement in this life, they seem to go on enjoying
themselves and prospering. There seems to be no justice.
But is this really so? We have to remind ourselves that
ultimately everything is under God's sovereign control.
This is a fact which few Christians would dispute, but I
wonder if we do not sometimes need to remind ourselves
of how far God's control extends. For instance, In Proverbs 16:33 we read that he controls the throw of a dice.
In other words, even the small and seemingly-random
things of life are in His hands. In Proverbs 16:4 we are
told that even the existence of the wicked fits into God's
final plans and purposes. In Proverbs 16:9 we read that all
the 'steps' or actions of man are planned by God. Think
about that for a moment. There is not a single thing anywhere on the face of the planet at any time that can be
said to be outside God's plans and purposes. There is no
power anywhere in the universe that can make God do
what he does not want to do or thwart His purposes in
any way.

The Lord does whatever pleases Him,
in the heavens and on the earth,
in the seas and all their depths.

(Psalm 135:6)

Despite what men may plan or do, God's plan for this
world is being worked out. Neither the scorn of unbelievers nor the rebellion of nations deters Him from His di-

vine purposes. The arrogance of puny men and their social agendas to throw off His rule elicits God's laughter (Psalm 2:4). This is not the derisory laughter of a tyrant, but the scorn of the Judge of all the earth at the wickedness of people who think they can escape an ultimate confrontation with Him.

But what about the bad things? Do they also fall under His rule? Are they not random slips that happen because of evil? Do they not come from the devil? If we agree that the bad things that happen in the world come from the devil in the sense that God is caught by surprise and cannot do anything about it, we would be admitting that God is not all-powerful or all-knowing. There would be moments when He would not know what the enemy is doing. If that were true, not only He but his entire universe would be strikingly vulnerable. There would be no ultimate security for the believer, because at any moment of divine unawareness the enemy could strike and victory would be his.

But we do not grant the devil that power. The account of Job is ever before us. Before the devil could touch God's servant, he needed divine permission. Even then his activities were under restraints. Job did not know or understand this, but we have the record. We are permitted a glimpse behind the scenes. Job, without knowing the dynamics of what was happening to him, was engulfed in tragedy and sorrow.

Thus we have to concede that in some mysterious way, without being tainted by evil himself, God is depicted as standing behind the evil things that happen in this world. Let me illustrate this from the Bible.

Take the matter of accidental and premature death. Is it possible for God's purposes to be seen in that?

However, if he does not do it intentionally,

but God lets it happen, he is to flee to a place
I will designate.

(Exodus 21: 13)

We are told that 'God lets it happen'. Does this not indicate His involvement? We must not make the mistake of excluding God's purposes from the tragedies of life.

The story of Ruth will be familiar to many. Here was a family that suffered misfortune and death. But see how Naomi interprets the events: '... the Lord's hand has gone out against me!' (Ruth 1:13). It was not that she was especially wicked. She had not done anything wrong any more than Job had. But steeped as she was in the history of her people, a history filled with divine sovereign intervention, she saw no contradiction in believing that God's purpose for her at this point in her life was tragedy. She did not take the sad event out of God's hands and place it in the hands of Satan. Rather, she saw what happened as coming from the hand of God. The same hand that sometimes deals with us in mercy, generosity and bounty can also 'go out against us'.

Even in matters of national interest, we see God at work. Isaiah was commissioned to preach to the disobedient people of God facing final disaster and exile. Could it happen that God would actually take protection from His people? Yes–even though they do not recognise him as God, He is still the Lord. He is the One in whose hands lie the destiny of nations. Thus, speaking through the prophet, God says:

I am the Lord, and there is no other.
I form the light and create darkness.
I bring prosperity and create disaster;
I, the Lord, do all these things.

(Isaiah 45:6–7)

Create disaster! Yes, that is what He says. That is how far His sovereign rule extends. It is true that men create their own disasters on earth, but ultimately nothing takes place, even in the international realm, without God's divine plan and permission.

Are we left then with no personal hope? Are we simply in the hands of the Almighty to suffer grief when He wills it or joy when He grants it? Is there an arbitrariness about God? Is He capricious? No. The prophet Jeremiah experienced the worst imaginable tragedy for the Jewish nation, the destruction of their city and temple, the death of thousands and the deportation of survivors. Yet he could say:

> Though He brings grief, He will show
>   compassion
> so great is His unfailing love.
> For He does not willingly bring affliction
> or grief to the children of men.
>   (Lamentations 3:32–33)

But is God in control of the sinful actions of men? We have to say that even the sinful deeds of human beings are not outside the scope of His sovereign rule. In 2 Samuel 24:1 we read that as part of His judgment against Israel, God incited David to do something wrong so that His purpose in chastisement could be displayed. Again in 1 Kings 22:21 we are told that God put a lying spirit into the mouths of the prophets because He had decreed disaster for them. What are we to make of these things?

Firstly, we need to bear in mind that human responsibility is never discounted. Whatever these strange Bible references may mean, they do not imply that man is an automaton in the hands of a supreme power, with no option but to sin and bring destruction on himself. Human beings are commanded to obey, choose and believe. They are held accountable. We have minds and wills.

Secondly, I can do no better than to refer to D A Carson who, in his book 'A Call to Spiritual Reformation', reminds us that God does not relate to good and evil in the same way. Carson points out that there are usually two mistakes people make when they grapple with the problem of evil. The first is to say that God is not involved with evil at all. It all comes from the devil. God has no part in it. The second error is to conclude that God is behind good and evil in exactly the same way.

The first error assumes that another power exists apart from God and outside the domain of His sovereignty. This dualistic view of the universe finds no support in Scripture. The second mistake maintains that what God ordains takes place and what God does not ordain does not take place. Therefore if both good and evil take place, it is because God has ordained both. Carson points out that if God stands behind good and evil in exactly the same way, He is entirely amoral. This means that, although God is powerful, He is not good.

> The Bible's witness will not let us accept either of these positions. The Bible insists God is sovereign, so sovereign that nothing that takes place in the universe can escape the outermost boundary of His control; yet the Bible insists God is good, unreservedly good, the very standard of goodness. We are driven to conclude that God does not stand behind good and evil in exactly the same way. In other words, He stands behind good and evil 'asymmetrically'. He stands behind good in such a way that the good can ultimately be credited to Him; He stands behind evil in

such a way that what is evil is inevitably cred-
ited to secondary agents and all their malig-
nant effects. They cannot escape His sway, in
exactly the same way that Satan has no power
over Job without God's sanction; yet God
remains mysteriously distant from the evil itself.

I say 'mysteriously' because how He does
this is mysterious, for reasons still to be explored. In fact, it is the very mysteriousness
of His control that prompts not a few biblical writers to wrestle in agony over the problem of evil—not only the writer of Job, but
Habakkuk, some of the psalmists, and others. (A Call to Spiritual Reformation, p. 158)

Still staying with Carson, whose book I heartily rec-
ommend to all thinking Christians, we need to reflect a
little further on the nature of God's sovereignty if we are
to receive comfort in the midst of tragedy, suffering and
grief. There are yet another two extremes to avoid. If God
were sovereign and nothing more, we would merely be in
the grip of raw power. There would be nothing we could
relate to. On the other hand, if God were personal and no
more it would be easier to relate to Him, but we would
see no sovereignty, power or transcendence.

Carson reminds us that the wonderful truth is that
God is both transcendent and personal. He is transcend-
ent in that He exists above and beyond time and space.
He is exalted and sovereignly rules over the works of His
hands. Yet He is personal and presents Himself to us as
Father and Lord.

All of my most meaningful relationships are
bound up with the fact that God has disclosed

Himself to be a person. (Ibid, p. 159)

This means that when Naomi lost first her husband and then her two sons, a personal God was involved, not some raw force that unfeelingly dealt the blow. When the 'Lord's hand went out against her', it was with divine purpose and compassion for a world that needed a Saviour. Naomi and her daughter-in-law Ruth were to be links in the chain (Ruth 4:13–22).

Can God be trusted? If He is only a transcendent force that arranges each event on the planet with no regard for good or evil, He cannot be trusted. But if He is not only sovereign and transcendent but also a Father who enters into our sufferings, then He can be trusted. If He exists and He is evil, then all we have left is a dismal fatalism as we wait for the next blow to fall. But if He exists and He is good, we must say that in spite of the difficulty in coping with or explaining the bad things that happen to us, behind all things is a good God whose ultimate purposes are good. Our limitations in seeing and understanding do not preclude us trusting Him. In the final analysis, what other viable option is there?

The same applies to our personal tragedies. They do not happen in a moment that is out of the control of the Almighty. They do not happen in a time of divine unawareness; nor are they the result of some cosmic struggle against evil when the forces of evil momentarily win. Without laying the blame for the evil acts of others at God's door as if He willed evil, we have to see His sovereign involvement without placing any guilt on Him. We know that God's purposes are always accomplished. But in Scripture His sovereignty is never presented in such a way that it leads to fatalism. Rather, it encourages us to see a glorious purpose being worked out.

People who are part of the plan cannot always see the

role they are playing. We now have the inspired record to study. We can see from Scripture how God's plans work out. Therefore God's dealings with us, however confusing and mysterious, lead us to trust Him and to pray to Him. It leads us to faith, the assurance that in some way unknown to us, 'in all things God works for the good of those who love Him, who have been called according to His purpose' (Romans 8:28).

We can trust God to be faithful. He will always be true to His nature. The last word in this section goes to D A Carson, whom I have already quoted liberally:

> Christians are prepared to accept certain mysteries. We confess that the Father is God, the Son is God, and the Holy Spirit is God—yet there is but one God. Christian thinkers across the ages have taken pains to show how there is no necessary contradiction in such an understanding of the trinitarian character of God, even if there are huge swaths of mystery involved. So also here: God is sovereign and transcendent, and He is personal.
>
> Perhaps it is the way God apparently stands outside time and space that enables Him to handle secondary causes the way He does. I do not know. What does time look like to a transcendent God? I do not know. I only know that the Bible speaks of His 'pre'destining power and His 'fore'ordination of events, even though these are categories of time. I suppose that if he is to communicate effectively with us, He must graciously stoop to use categories that we can understand. But despite all the mysteries bound up with the nature of God, I perceive, on the

basis of Scripture, that He is simultaneously personal and transcendent. He is utterly sovereign over His created order, yet He is nothing less than personal as He deals with me. Sometimes it is more important to worship such a God than to understand Him.

The Joseph Principle

Few Christians will be unfamiliar with the story of Joseph. Most of us have had occasion at some point in our lives to quote Genesis 50:19–20:

> But Joseph said to them, 'Don't be afraid. Am I in the place of God? You intended to harm me, but God intended it for good to accomplish what is now being done, the saving of many lives.'

This well-known story is still a brilliant illustration of the principles we have been discussing. It shows how good and evil fit together in God's plan. Joseph's personal history was one of almost unremitting bad experiences. No doubt his youthful pride and his father's overt favouritism played a role in his brothers' response to him, but it must have been a great shock to be kidnapped, imprisoned in a pit and sold as a slave. His years of service in Potiphar's household were followed by a term of imprisonment. Worse still was the fact that he was unjustly accused. Have you ever wondered how Joseph felt? What were his emotions, thoughts and responses to God during this period of his life? Did he question God? Did he panic and give in to despair? Was his trauma of slavery and imprisonment any better or worse than the assault on our emotions in our own tragedies? The problem with characters like

Joseph is that it is hard to humanise them. The stories seem so mythical and far away. Yet he was a real man with real feelings. Remember how he broke down and wept when he saw his brothers (Genesis 45:1–2)? We all marvel at God's great wisdom in overruling the wickedness of men and so engineering circumstances that Joseph became a ruler in Egypt. But can He not do the same for us? Can He not so work in our circumstances that what has happened to us may yet be seen to redound to His own great glory?

Think of what was accomplished by all the things Joseph experienced. Firstly, a pagan people heard and saw faith in the true God displayed. That faith had a profound impact on Pharaoh (Genesis 41:37–40). Secondly, whole nations were saved from starvation in a time of dreadful famine. The Hebrew race itself was preserved because, unknown to them, one of their sons had risen to a place of prominence in the Egyptian kingdom. Thirdly, the whole history of the exodus with its drama, awesome displays of divine power and its motif of redemption were prepared by Joseph being sold as a slave into Egypt. It does appear that Joseph was conscious of a divine plan for his life (Genesis 37:5–11). Yet is it not possible that, like you and me, he was called upon to trust God when the way seemed dark and dreary?

In this wonderful illustration of God's sovereignty, the actions of Joseph's brothers or any of the other wicked people in the story are never attributed to God. They are accountable for their own deeds. God stands in such a relationship to evil that it is not outside of His rule yet He cannot be held responsible for it. On the other hand, the good in the story is clearly attributed to God. 'You intended to harm me, but God intended it for good' (Genesis 50:20). God proves His faithfulness to His own nature and His care and concern for His people.

A Christian response to tragedy

Because God remains faithful, we can continue to trust Him. Putting our trust in Him and depending on His intrinsic goodness frees us from the need to find explanations for everything. It also frees us to admit that often we are perplexed. Being a Christian does not mean that you have an answer for everything. Job was perplexed because he could see no discernible reason for what happened to him. Yet when God revealed His greatness and power to Job, it not only satisfied him but made him feel ashamed of the way he had dealt with his tragedy.

> My ears had heard of you
> but now my eyes have seen you.
> Therefore I despise myself
> and repent in dust and ashes.
> (Job 42:5–6)

The psalmist was honest enough to admit his deep perplexity and depression:

> Why are you downcast, O my soul?
> Why so disturbed within me?
>
> (Psalm 43:5)

Yet for all that, there was still the sure knowledge that God was his Saviour:

> Put your hope in God
> for I will yet praise him
> my Saviour and my God.
>
> (Psalm 43:5)

We also do not deny our pain. It is a cruel and needless teaching that makes Christians feel that they should be above it all and be constantly rejoicing. There is a unhappy superficiality in those who refuse to admit that they are sad or that life is sometimes sad. According to King David, when God seems to hide his face, we are dismayed (Psalm 30:7). There is an inner pain, a dismay at life, when God seems to withdraw and the shadow of affliction falls over us. It is true that 'rejoicing comes in the morning', but it is also true that 'weeping remains for the night' (Psalm 30:5). We freely acknowledge our perplexity and pain at the inexplicable things that happen to us. We grieve and hurt and feel as all other people do. There is however an added factor in the Christian's response to life's tragedies. We wait on God. We know that He is our Father. He will make His purposes and plans come to pass. We may never know the full story here on earth, but we are confident that nothing happens randomly and without purpose. We do not waste our energy on unanswerable questions, but at the same time we remain alert to learn what lesson we can from what has happened to us. We do not react in haste. We do not seek for vengeance if someone has harmed us.

We do, of course, seek justice if that is possible in our situation. We know that often those who harm us get away with it. Without our hope in a personal God, we would despair. But we know that a day is coming when God Himself will take vengeance on our behalf.

He will dispense justice, and no one will escape. This is what the perplexed psalmist came to understand:

When I tried to understand all this,
it was oppressive to me
till I entered the sanctuary of God;
then I understood their final destiny.
Surely you place them on slippery ground;

you cast them down to ruin.
How suddenly are they destroyed,
completely swept away by terrors!
As a dream when one awakes,
so when you arise, O Lord,
you will despise them as fantasies.
                              (Psalm 73:16–20)

Finally, as Christians we enjoy the peace that passes understanding. This is a real aspect of an experience with God. He does not leave us without comfort. He places within us an assurance that all is under His divine control. Freed from the need for revenge, from the need for explanations and from the throttling grip of bitterness, we are able to leave things with Him and be content. Can God be trusted? Yes, He can. His ways are hidden from us, but He has revealed His character to us so that we may know Him.

4

The Truth About Trials

I stood on her doorstep with not a word to say. I felt quite overwhelmed by the magnitude of her tragedy and was too young and inexperienced to know what to do.

About two weeks previously I had entered a bank. She and the bank manager were having a loud discussion. She was fortyish, stout and bedraggled. Because the altercation was public, it was not hard to distinguish the facts. Her husband had died unexpectedly quite recently and an insurance policy had paid out a fairly substantial sum of money. She was obviously in an extremely depressed state be cause of what had happened and in this condition had decided to withdraw all the money and blow it on a spending spree. The bank manager was trying to talk her out of it, but she insisted on having the money. Her young teenage son, embarrassed by all the public attention, was standing to one side.

Because I was behind her in the queue, I broke into the conversation.

'Excuse me,' I said with youthful enthusiasm that sees nothing wrong with interfering in other people's business, 'I'm the minister of a church in the area. If I can be of help, I would be glad to make myself available.'

Needless to say, I was almost totally ignored and finally I left after being helped by one of the clerks. The woman and the bank manager were still loudly debating her decision to draw the money.

Two weeks later I was doing door-to-door evangelism. I came to a dingy, rundown cottage with an over-grown garden and knocked at the door. I was amazed to see this very woman standing in front of me. She stood staring vacantly at me, looking as bedraggled and unkempt as before. I struggled for a moment to place where I had seen her before, then I remembered the scene in the bank.

I introduced myself.

'I've met you before,' I said.

She nodded.

'You're the lady who lost her husband two months ago.'

Again she nodded, looking as vacant and dull as it is possible to be.

Searching for something else to say and because I was responsible for the youth work at our church, I said, 'How is your son?'

'He died yesterday,' she said in a monotone and closed the door.

Our personal tragedies raise a number of important questions. Why did it happen? Is God angry with me? What have I done to deserve this? Our agony is deepened if we have been led to believe that, because we are Christians, something is terribly wrong if any thing bad happens to us. We feel offended with God. We feel as if he has made an error of judgement and treated us unfairly.

Some Christian teaching has erred greatly by becoming too triumphalistic. People are taught that this world is to be the scene of one victory after another over the powers of darkness. The powers of darkness express their destructive purposes in sicknesses and ailments. Thus sickness, trouble and affliction in its many forms is to be resisted and rebuked. Each problem is seen as a deliberate ploy of the devil to ensnare the believer into the bondage of fear and misery.

This teaching has focused attention again on the vital

area of faith and trust. It has emphasised our need to believe in a supernatural God who is above the laws of nature. It encourages a trust in him in all the everyday affairs of life. All this is very positive.

Unfortunately this school of thought refuses to recognise the clear teaching of Scripture about the weakness and vulnerability of the human condition. Trouble-free living is not the lot of the children of Adam, even when they become the children of God, for 'we must go through many hardships to enter the kingdom of God' (Acts 14:22). Many sincere Christians have been grievously wounded by being led to expect healing or deliverance in this world, while this will be ours in fullness only in the next world. Wrong expectations of God can lead to much disillusionment, depression and disappointment.

But though there may be those who are mistaken in this regard, there are still the agonies that come upon us because of the experiences of life. When the massacre took place in our church, a stunned nation asked why. Embodied in this question were several others. Why did the perpetrators choose a church? What did this mean for churches in South Africa? What was it saying about the attitude of liberation movements to evangelical churches? What was it about the church that invited an attack of this nature? But the great question that was being asked in a hundred different way was, 'Why did God allow it?'

Why does God allow anything? The loss of a husband and a son within the space of two months; the loss of a spouse to someone else; the violation of a daughter; the crumbling of a business empire; the frustration of perpetual sickness in the family. In fact, why does God allow trials at all? There are several truths about trials that need to be restated. What follows is not all there is to be said about trials, but simply some principles that all who face tragedy and suffering need to think through.

Trials are inescapable

Many things in life are uncertain but one thing of which we can be certain is that difficulties and trials will come. Eliphaz , one of Job's comforters, said to him:

> For hardship does not spring from the soil,
> nor does trouble sprout from the ground.
> Yet man is born to trouble
> as surely as sparks fly upward.
>
> (Job 5:6–7)

In other words, the principle of trouble and hardship is built into our fallen world and none escape it although some may experience more of it than others. One of Job's replies to his friends confirms this gloomy fact in a classic passage often quoted at funeral services:

> Man born of woman
> is of few days and full of trouble.
> He springs up like a flower and withers away;
> like a fleeting shadow, he does not endure.
>
> (Job 14:1–2)

We do not need to turn to the Scriptures to convince us of this; any observation of life will confirm the fact that life, as a rule, is not easy.

> Care lives with all; no rules, no precepts save
> The wise from woe, no fortitude the brave:
> Grief is to man as certain as the grave:
> Tempests and storms in life's whole progress
>   rise,
> And hope shines dimly through o'erclouded
>   skies;

Some drops of comfort on the favour'd fall,
But showers of sorrow are the lot of all.
                    (Crabbe, The Library)

A fact that we constantly need to keep before us is
that Christians are also part of this world. We must remember the warning of Jesus in John 16:33: 'In this world you
will have trouble'. In Acts 14:22 the apostles reminded the
new followers of Jesus that 'we must go through many hardships to enter the kingdom of God'.

In the final great panorama of redemption described in
the book of Revelation, we are reminded that those who are
before the throne of God and who have washed their robes
in the blood of the Lamb are those who have come out of
the great tribulation (Revelation 7:1 4). Contrary to much
popular teaching today, the tribulation does not refer to a
compressed time of extraordinary persecution right at the
end of world history, but rather to 'this' world, its spirit and
mentality, where all Christians live. The world is a place of
tribulation and suffering. The suffering endured by Christians may at times take the form of persecution, but by and
large it is part of the 'showers of sorrow' that are the lot of
all.

This is a far cry from those who would have us believe
that our lives as Christians on this earth should be one constant march of triumph and trouble-free living, where the
pressures and fears and struggles common to all are somehow prevented from affecting believers . The Bible is full of
examples of God's people under pressure. Listen to David
in Psalm 6:

O Lord, do not rebuke me in your anger
or discipline me in your wrath.
Be merciful to me, Lord, for I am faint;
O Lord, heal me, for my bones are in agony.

My soul is in anguish.
How long, O Lord, how long?

I am worn out from groaning;
all night long I flood my bed with weeping;
and drench my couch with tears.
My eyes grow weak with sorrow;
they fail because of all my foes.

(Psalm 6:1–3, 6–7)

Is it possible for God's servants to reach such depths of sorrow that they are 'worn out from groaning' and 'flood [their] bed with weeping'? Yes, it is. But we must not forget that there is another side to this sorrow. In Psalm 6:9, David says:

The Lord has heard my cry for mercy;
the Lord accepts my prayer.

Jesus said: 'But take heart! I have overcome the world' (John 16:33). The Lord's help and the message of hope for the believer under stress is all gloriously true. My aim in this chapter is, however, to counter the popular notion that Christians should enjoy a trouble-free existence. If we truly believed that we are not exonerated from troubles in this world, we would not be confused when they come. Bishop J C Ryle comments on David's words in 2 Samuel 23:4–5:

He is like the light of the morning at sunrise
on a cloudless morning,
like the brightness after rain
that brings the grass from the earth.
Is not my house right with God?
Has He not made with me an everlasting
        covenant,

arranged and secured in every part?
Will He not bring to fruition my salvation
and grant me my very desire?

He writes:

Poor David might well say this! If ever there
was a man whose house was full of trials, and
whose life was full of sorrows, that man was
David. Trials from the envy of his own breth-
ren, trials from the unjust persecution of Saul,
trials from his own servants, such as Joab and
Ahithophel, trials from a wife, even that
Michal who once loved him so much, trials
from his children, such as Absalom, Amnon,
and Adonijah, trials from his own subjects,
who at one time forgot all he had done, and
drove him out of Jerusalem by rebellion, trials of all kinds, wave upon wave, were con-
tinually breaking on David to the very end
of his days. Some of the worst of these trials,
no doubt, were the just consequences of his
own sins, and the wise chastisement of a loving Father. But we must have hard hearts if
we do not feel that David was indeed 'a man
of sorrows'.

But is not this the experience of many of
God's noblest saints and dearest children?
What careful reader of the Bible can fail to
see that Adam, and Noah, and Abraham, and
Isaac, and Jacob, and Joseph, and Moses, and
Samuel, were all men of many sorrows, and
that those sorrows chiefly arose out of their
own homes?

(The Upper Room, p. 256)

These are wise words and Christians today would do well to reflect on them.

Who is responsible for our suffering?

H L Mencken was probably the most influential US journalist in the 1920s. The following quotation is attributed to him:

> The act of worship as carried on by Christians, seems to me to be debasing rather than ennobling. It involves grovelling before a Being who, if He really exists, deserves to be denounced instead of respected.

This comment warrants some thought. If God truly exists and merely brings suffering upon us out of some spiteful and malicious motive, then truly such a being should be denounced. If there were no ultimate good, no purpose or plan at work in the world, then we worship in vain. But we know differently. We have not been left without light. We know that divine purposes are being worked out in our universe. We also know that God is good in spite of the evil we see around us. Mencken is wrong because his understanding of God and the universe are wrong. But it still leaves the question unanswered. Where does suffering come from? Who is responsible for it?

Let me suggest four causes of the hurt, pain, alienation and suffering we experience in our world. In the first place, we must remember that 'we live in an imperfect world'. As explained earlier, this world is fallen. It is not what it was when it left the hand of God. A universal alienation between God and creation took place. We fell from a state of perfection to a new condition of basic enmity between man and God. Now, instead of eating of the fruits of the garden, man would earn his food with painful toil among thorns and thistles (Genesis 3:17–18). Now, instead of harmonious relationships and the joy of family life, pain would increase in child-bearing; a new dynamic would be introduced into human relationships and a new hierarchy would be established (Genesis 3:16). In other words, the stage was set for all the disharmony and acrimony that we are familiar with today . In addition, death was introduced. Not a mere sudden striking down in judgment but rather a principle of decay and decline.

The whole sad saga of human folly slowly unravels before us as we read the Bible, until we reach the epitome of human rebellion and alienation in Psalm 2:1–3:

> Why do the nations conspire
> and the people plot in vain?
> The kings of the earth take their stand
> and the rulers gather together against the
> Lord
> and against his Anointed One.
> 'Let us break their chains,' they say,
> 'and throw off their fetters.'

Toil, thorns, rage, plotting, rebellion and anarchy is the lot of this world. All wars, disease, sickness, death and even natural disasters can be traced back to that one act of representative disobedience in Eden. Paul tells us something surprising about creation in Romans 8:19–21:

> The creation waits in eager expectation for
> the sons of God to be revealed. For the crea-
> tion was subjected to frustration, not by its
> own choice, but by the will of the one who

subjected it, in hope that the creation itself
will be liberated from its bond age of decay
and brought into the glorious freedom of the
children of God.

In other words, the whole of creation has been frustrated by man's disobedience and longs for the day when the children of God will be glorified. At that time creation itself will undergo a regeneration and be freed from the curse placed on it at the fall.

So much of what we suffer today is part of the consequence of living in a fallen world among fallen people with imperfect ideas, plans and limited abilities. James reminds us that we will 'face trials of many kinds' (James 1:2). He was thinking primarily of the suffering brought upon believers by persecution, but there are many kinds of trials. Some of our suffering will certainly be persecution, but it will also include the tribulation and affliction that is part of what it means to be human.

Let us turn, in the second place, to the kind of suffering that we experience 'because of our faith'. We must remind ourselves that this is something we ought to expect in this world.

Blessed are those who are persecuted
because of righteousness
for theirs is the kingdom of heaven.
'Blessed are you when people insult you, persecute you and falsely say all kinds of evil against you because of me. Rejoice and be glad, because great is your reward in heaven, for in the same way they persecuted the prophets who were before you.'
(Matthew 5:10–12)

Being persecuted for righteousness' sake is the experience of many believers. Missionary organisations constantly filter through reports of believers who have been killed in some countries for the crime of believing in Jesus Christ. For many reading this book, that kind of extreme persecution will not form part of their experience. Most probably the suffering they endure for Jesus' sake will be the more covert kind of family ostracism or displeasure, domestic break-up or job discrimination. But it is true that sometimes we are called to walk a lonely road because we believe in Christ and for no other reason.

After the massacre at our church, many people sent us messages bearing the slogan 'the blood of the martyrs is the seed of the church'. They immediately assumed that we were being persecuted for our faith. We do not believe that the violence that erupted on that fateful night was persecution for our faith. Nor do we see ourselves as martyrs in any way. We see ourselves simply as the victims of violence. We do not see what happened to us as being any worse than what has been happening in the townships of our land before and since the attack on our church.

We were at great pains to make this clear to the media who were watching to see how we would react to the worldwide outcry at the atrocity in our church while devastating violence takes place on a daily basis in other parts of our land without eliciting the same response. There was of course a very sinister element in our case. The attack on a group of worshippers introduced a new twist to a culture of violence. No place was safe anymore. There was no respect for God. As in the scene described in Psalm 2, the nations were raging and the people were plotting; a fist was shaken in the face of God. A new form of cruelty was introduced into the South African situation.

But we see all this as a fairly predictable outcome of

the liberation struggle which has included a call to violence on the part of several prominent church leaders. A reinterpretation of the gospel by liberation theologians has abandoned the spirit of Christ for the spirit of Marx. Guns are put into the hands of youth who form roving bands of criminals. Their higher authorities often lose control of them. High on drugs, these groups attack 'soft' targets. St James Church presented such a soft target—a quiet suburb on a stormy Sunday night. Demonic and outrageous as this atrocity was, our congregation did not see it as an act of persecution but as a random criminal act of people under the mistaken notion that they were working for liberation. We do, however, need to remember that in other cases suffering and disaster may indeed overtake us because we belong to Christ.

There is a third possible explanation for the troubles we experience in life. 'We may bring them upon ourselves'. Notice Peter's warning to us:

> If you are insulted because of the name of Christ, you are blessed, for the Spirit of glory and of God rests on you. If you suffer, it should not be as a murderer or thief or any other kind of criminal, or even as a meddler.
> (1 Peter 4:14–15)

Kenneth Wuest says that the word 'meddler' means 'a self-appointed overseer in others' matters' (Word Studies, 1 Peter, p. 121). The truth is that it is possible to incur the wrath and dislike of others and even to cause alienation in relationships because of our own demeanour. This is stressed in an even more graphic manner in Proverbs 18:6–7:

> A fool's lips bring him strife,

and his mouth invites a beating.
A fool's mouth is his undoing,
and his lips are a snare to his soul.

If our own short tempers or interfering mannerisms cause people to react to us, we are not to assume that we are suffering for Christ's sake. In fact Peter lumps this kind of inconsiderate behaviour together with that of murderers, thieves and criminals. In other words, just as more obvious kinds of antisocial behaviour cause distress and harm and finally bring 'suffering' upon the person, and justly so, so does a behaviour pattern that presumes to know everything and to tell others how to handle their affairs.

Many people today are lonely and bitter, thinking that all the world is against them. But this is because they have sharp, critical tongues and intimidating attitudes. No one can bear to be in their company too long because their very presence is oppressive. They are their own worst enemy and the real tragedy lies in the fact that they cannot see it. They mistakenly feel that they are being persecuted for some righteous cause.

There is a fourth solemn cause for some of the tribulations we endure as Christians. This is 'the discipline that comes from the Father's hand'. Like our own children who constantly need guidance and correction when they are growing up, so we sometimes need the heavenly Father's intervention when we stray in disobedience. The classic passage of Scripture dealing with this is Hebrews 12:4–12:

In your struggle against sin, you have not yet resisted to the point of shedding your blood. And you have forgotten that word of encouragement that addresses you as sons:

'My son, do not make light of the
Lord's discipline,
and do not lose heart when He rebukes you,
because the Lord disciplines those He loves
and punishes everyone He accepts as a son.'

Endure hardship as discipline; God is treating you as sons. For what son is not disciplined by his father? If you are not disciplined (and everyone undergoes discipline), then you are illegitimate children and not true sons. Moreover, we have all had human fathers who disciplined us and we respected them for it. How much more should we submit to the Father of our spirits and live! Our fathers disciplined us for a little while as they thought best; but God disciplines us for our good, that we may share his holiness . No discipline seems pleasant at the time, but painful. Later on, however, it produces a harvest of righteousness and peace for those who have been trained by it. Therefore, strengthen your feeble arms and weak knees!

When God deals with us through chastisement He does so, not because He hates us, but because He loves us. If He sent His Son to die for us and to bear our guilt on the cross, will he not with Christ give us all things (Romans 8:32)? He will most assuredly see to it that his true children are led and guided into increasing holiness.

The Scripture is quite plain in its statements about discipline. None of it seems pleasant at the time (Hebrews 12:11). On the contrary, it is painful. It is this very pain that we all seek to escape. Yet it is essential to the later harvest of righteousness and peace to be garnered in our lives.

God's discipline, we are told, is fair and good. His intention is that we may share in his holiness. In other words, He is preparing us for the ultimate consummation of our faith when we will be with Him forever. While we are on earth, we are being trained. God sometimes uses the unpleasant experiences of life as His training tools. This is expressed in Psalm 119 in this way:

> Before I was afflicted I went astray,
> but now I obey your word.
> It is good for me to be afflicted
> so that I might learn your decrees.
> (Psalm 119:67, 71)

Affliction has a way of sharpening our senses and enabling us to make new assessments. Our priorities are quickly rearranged in an emergency. You may have experienced this in your own case. When death or tragedy strikes, for instance, it makes us realise again how fragile life is. We reflect on its shortness and its uncertainties. We begin to ask ourselves what are the really important things.

On the night of the tragedy in our church, many people were shocked by the realisation that they could have been killed so very unexpectedly. This caused them to examine their relationship with God. Some people surrendered their lives to Christ and became Christians for the first time. They realised they were only nominal in their Christian faith. Others who had been slipping away spiritually and had become careless suddenly woke up to their danger. Maybe something similar has happened to you or your family. You were going astray but now you obey His Word. Now you are learning His decrees in a way you would not have appreciated before.

On the night of our tragedy people clung to each other in a new way. Family suddenly became important and

friendships took on new meaning. Small and petty things
that so often disrupt our relationships were showed up
for what they are and were swiftly abandoned. No wonder the writer of Hebrews said, 'do not lose heart when
He rebukes you'.

The difficulty of course is to determine when discipline is taking place. This is a very difficult subject and is
best left for the believer Himself to assess. When God is
teaching us something, we all know it. There is after all a
spiritual instinct in all of us who are part of God's flock.
John 10:3 reminds us that the sheep know the Shepherd's
voice. We know when He is speaking to us. Nevertheless
there may be confusion for a while during the suffering
we endure. We cannot always discern things and make
accurate judgements immediately. Often it needs to be
done in retrospect. Dr Peter Masters makes some helpful
suggestions in an article entitled 'How can we tell the
Lord's disciplines?' (The Sword and the Trowel, p. 7). In
it he suggests that we look for three things. Firstly, we
should try to remember if there have been any milder disciplines in our lives. In other words, have we received gentle
warnings from the Lord over a period of time. In Hebrews 12:5 we see that there is discipline before there is
rebuke. Look for a gradation in God's dealings with you.
Have our spiritual joys been crushed? Have worldly and
materialistic desires been frustrated?

Secondly, Masters suggests that we ascertain whether
the event happening in our life is kind. God's dealings
with us, however severe, are not hostile or cruel. Sometimes our sins and backsliding bring fearful consequences
upon us, but God never abandons the stance of 'love'.

Thirdly, we need to remember that a chastening is
always reversible. Trial comes to an end. It is always only
'for a while'. When there has been heart-searching and
repentance, mercy and restoration follow. Much may be

lost in the process of chastisement, but finally our relationship with God is restored.

Having said all this, we must be sensitive to the suffering of others and not jump to hasty conclusions. While it may be true that God is dealing in love with His children, it may be equally true that they are suffering the afflictions common to all who live in this fallen world. We would do well to keep our opinions to ourselves and to wait for clearer light before we draw conclusions about the things that happen to us or to others.

This raises another matter that needs reflection. Christians are usually more sensitive to the things that befall them than unbelievers. This is because we are prone to draw lessons from the things that happen to us. We immediately look for some spiritual significance in the vicissitudes of life. We want to know what God is saying to us. All who truly love the Saviour dread the thought that they have displeased Him in some way or unknowingly disobeyed Him. They therefore react to suffering with a peculiar sensitivity not always understood by others.

This needs to be carefully appreciated. For those who live daily with the sense of God's presence, nothing could be worse than suddenly to be bereft of it. We would rather suffer in some other way than forfeit the sense of God's favour. This is most commendable and needs to be encouraged for it is a value sadly lacking in our world.

However, this very sensitivity carries its own danger. We tend sometimes to read spiritual significance into life's events too quickly. We are in danger of becoming pious and superstitious. We also run the danger of misrepresenting our Master to those around us. He may be represented as an overly sensitive ogre who is offended the minute we make a mistake. We must avoid this because we know it is not true. God loves us with an everlasting love. His love is greater than our mistakes and offences. It is a love that has carried all our sins—past, present and future—to the cross. It is a love that may discipline us but will never abandon us. Let us represent Him accurately.

Trials are a test of faith

We have often heard people use phrases loosely like 'my faith is being tested'. Is this true? If so, what does it mean? Let us look first at 1 Peter 1:7:

> These have come so that your faith—of greater worth than gold, which perishes even though refined by fire—may be proved genuine and may result in praise, glory and honour when Jesus Christ is revealed.

Here we are told that our faith is of greater value than gold. This is a way of saying that the most important thing about our relationship with God is our faith. He is determined to strengthen and test it. Nothing is more important. There are two good reasons for this.

Firstly, faith is the act that binds us to God. Faith, as trust in Christ, is the basis on which we are accepted into His family. So me people speak of faith as if faith itself is the important thing. But for the Christian it is not the mere fact of possessing faith that counts, but rather the object in which our faith is placed. Therefore it is faith 'in Christ' that matters. With the rise of religious pluralism, it is important to make this distinction. Increasingly we are being made aware of other faiths and religious systems which are syncretistic in nature and can accommodate all other faiths. For the Christian this is unacceptable.

The world has moved away from objective facts into the

uncertain world of subjective verification. The result is that whatever is true for you is truth. It does not need to be verified. Verification in fact is not even desirable because it leads to arrogance and dogmatism. The world's view is that it doesn't matter whether it is true or not. What matters is that it works for you. But for the believer in Christ this is simply not sufficient. Our faith must be rooted somewhere. We place it in the great historical fact of Christ and His substitutionary death on the cross. Thus we stand anchored to a great event that took place in time and history. We trust in the true God of the universe.

But the second reason why our faith in Christ is so important to God is because it is so easily imitated. Throughout the Bible we are warned of those who are part of the Christian fellowship here on earth but do not possess saving faith. Moses warned against false prophets:

> You may say to yourselves, 'How can we know when a message has not been spoken by the Lord?' If what a prophet proclaims in the name of the Lord does not take place or come true, that is a message the Lord has not spoken. That prophet has spoken presumptuously. Do not be afraid of him.
>
> (Deuteronomy 18:21–22)

Jesus warned us:

> Not everyone who says to me, 'Lord, Lord,' will enter the kingdom of heaven, but only he who does the will of my Father who is in heaven. Many will say to me on that day, 'Lord, Lord, did we not prophesy in your name, and in your name drive out demons

and perform many miracles?' Then I will tell them plainly, 'I never knew you. Away from me, you evildoers!'

(Matthew 7:21–23)

Paul warned us:

Keep watch over yourselves and all the flock of which the Holy Spirit has made you overseers. Be shepherds of the church of God, which He bought with His own blood. I know that after I leave, savage wolves will come in among you and will not spare the flock. Even from your own number men will arise and distort the truth in order to draw away disciples after them. So be on your guard! Remember that for three years I never stopped warning each of you night and day with tears.

(Acts 20:28–31)

A number of the epistles of the New Testament contain long sections warning us of false believers who undermine the authority against the apostles, the way of salvation, and true Christian living. True saving faith binds us to Christ as a Person, whereas false faith embraces the system rather than the Person. Yet the false is often hard to detect. False believers are not easily rooted out and when they are identified, they are difficult to confront because they usually say all the right things.

How then is the genuine ever to be distinguished from the false? How do we know that we ourselves are not deluded? How do we prove that the faith we have is real and not imagined? The answer is that the difference between the true and the false is usually clearly seen in times of suffering. We need to remember this.

Suffering is sometimes the only platform on which God's grace has an opportunity to perform. Our natural response to trial, tragedy and suffering is to reject it. We see these things as unwelcome intruders. We want them banished from our lives. But unbelievers often see a ray of hope for themselves only after they have seen true Christian assurance displayed in the life of a believer in affliction. Joni Erikson Tada writes, 'I do not care if I am confined to this wheelchair provided from it I can bring glory to God' (A Step Further, p. 41). True children of God experience things in times of suffering that others do not. While all who experience tragedy are forced to reflection on life, only those who know God through Christ experience His supernatural power to keep them. The reason is that in times of great trial, God is especially close to His people. There is a special grace that is given to those who go through the furnace of affliction.

It was while he was being stoned that Stephen saw 'heaven open and the Son of Man standing at the right hand of God' (Acts 7:56). He was not granted this vision before, but in the moment of trial and death, this grace was given to him. So too with the three Israelites who were thrown into the fiery furnace. It was only when they were in the furnace that the mysterious fourth person was observed with them (Daniel 3:25). The prophet Isaiah gives the promise of God:

> When you pass through the waters,
> I will be with you;
> and when you pass through the rivers,
> they will not sweep over you.
> When you walk through the fire,

you will not be burned;
the flames will not set you ablaze.

(Isaiah 43:2)

God's presence is with us in a special way when we pass through the water and walk through the fire. We cannot expect the same measure of grace on a day-to-day basis for we walk by faith not by sight, but in times of great stress the Good Shepherd of the sheep draws near.

No doubt many of you have experienced this in your own great trials. We certainly did in ours. In fact it was a source of wonder and mystery to the media. In the midst of all the trauma and stress of those days, the bereaved were able to speak of peace, strength and an overwhelming sense of God's presence. Our church services were full of it. A month after the event, the newspapers phoned the church to check if people were still feeling the same way. Members of the congregation were able to extend forgiveness to the perpetrators and face the future with calm assurance. In fact I myself was hard pressed to answer media queries because I attempted to be honest. I wanted to give a credible account of how people were feeling. I wanted to be able to tell of little human failures to make the story more credible to an unbelieving world. But I honestly could not find one account of God's children being abandoned or comfortless. Those were high days for us.

I do not want to give the impression that there was no sense of suffering, grief or loss. But somehow we felt we were soaring. We were being carried into realms we had not entered before. We were passing through the waters and God was with us. We were walking through the fire and we were not burned. Of course there were tears and trauma and yes, there was stress and anguish, but we seemed to have a divine buffer during those days.

I have often said that if we were to plan to reach the country with the gospel, we would probably invite Billy Graham to visit and conduct mammoth televised crusades. Left to us, that would be the sort of plan we would devise. But God chose something different. He chose to put His suffering people on display. Evangelical Christians were on show before the world and the gospel was seen for what it is truly worth.

On other occasions of violence in our country, leaders called for retaliation of some sort and screamed slogans at the people. The sufferers at St James were given the supreme privilege of presenting Christ to the world as the true Shepherd of the sheep. May God give us grace to see our sufferings in a new light—as an opportunity to show off His grace, not as an event to be avoided at all costs.

A bag of gold

I cannot end this chapter without making one more observation about trials in the life of the believer. Trials do not change your spiritual status. If you are a true believer before you suffer, you will be one afterwards. Jesus went so far as to say that when we endure suffering and abuse for His sake, we are actually numbered with the prophets (Matthews 5:12). That is to say that we carry a similar status to them. We are in good company, for that is what the prophets suffered too.

The problem arises because, in their confusion, many true Christians feel that God is in some way indicating His anger with them when in fact it may be nothing of the kind. Even in a matter of divine discipline, we need to remember that God is still dealing with us as 'sons' (Hebrews 12:6–7). He is still our Father. His interest in us is still one of parental love. We must not lose sight of God's loving interest in His children even in the midst of life's severest trials, when all seems dark and stormy and we can see no light at the end of the tunnel. We must remember that the storm does pass and we remain His own possession, His family.

If two children are playing in a public park and they begin to squabble and an adult takes one child aside to remonstrate with him, what does that tell you? It tells you that the child who is rebuked is loved. He is a son. The other is not, he belongs to someone else We must learn to detect God's love and faithfulness even in the trials of life and remember that He can always be trusted.

Far from indicating that you are not a true Christian, trials and suffering prove that you are. 'For what son is not disciplined by his father?' (Hebrews 12:7). In fact, a trouble-free life is more of a danger sign than a trial-free life. 'If you are not disciplined (and everyone undergoes discipline), then you are illegitimate children and not true sons' (verse 8). When difficulties come we tend to brood and sometimes even to sink into self-pity. If you are going to brood, then brood about the right thing. Ask yourself, 'What can I discern of God's love in all this?'

Let us turn to a teacher from the past to learn from his wisdom. William Bridge was a Puritan preacher in London in the seventeenth century. He wrote a great Christian classic entitled 'A Lifting up for the Downcast'. In it he comments that often in times of affliction men dwell on the pain and discomfort, the hurt and the sorrow. They seldom look to see what mercies are hidden in their trials and sufferings. He illustrates this in the following manner.

Supposing a son asks his father for some money and his father, standing on a balcony or at a high window, throws down a bag of gold to him. Instead of catching it, the bag lands on his son's head and causes a small wound and some pain. If the son concentrates on his discomfort and pain and looks only at the bag that caused the pain, he will be ungrateful and angry. But if he looks into the bag and sees the large amount of gold his father has given him, he is filled with gratitude, forgets his pain and speaks well of his father.

Then Bridge adds this:

> Affliction is a bag of gold given to the people of God: though it seems like nothing more than a leather bag on the outside, there is gold within. So long as they stand poring over the leather bag, or dwell upon their affliction, they will never be thankful. They will never praise the Lord but instead are greatly discouraged. But if only they would look into the bag and count their gold then their discouragement would give way to comfort. I tell you from the Lord, there is gold within; look in this bag, the bag of affliction; count over all the gold which the Lord has given you in this affliction and then you will be quiet. If a mercy is taken from you, consider the burden that is taken away too. If some trial comes upon you, consider the mercy that comes with it. Labour ever, labour to see both together. See what is 'for' you as well as what is against you, then you will never lose courage although your affliction be ever so great.
>
> (A Lifting up of the Downcast, p.211–212)

Dear friends, never forget—there is gold in the bag!

5

Rebuilding your confidence

The loss of confidence after a traumatic event is a well-known phenomenon. It is easily observed in the ongoing course of life. In very minor events, for instance a bad fall off a bicycle, a child simply needs to be coaxed back onto it again. A more serious trauma such as a messy divorce may leave the remaining spouse with a great loss of self-esteem. If she needs to find a job after years as a housewife and homemaker, her lack of confidence can be even more painful. A motor car accident or a swimming accident or any other event that leads to trauma can lead to loss of confidence and an uncertainty as to how to proceed.

Christians do not escape the consequences of trauma. After the massacre in our church, one of the most common complaints by Christians was 'I can't pray'. Maybe you have felt the same way. Your old confidence in going to God in prayer has deserted you. Others in our fellowship experienced additional guilt feelings either because they were not there on the night, because they were not injured while others were, or because they reacted with more fear than others did. They carried this guilt into their prayer life and felt ashamed, confused and even betrayed by God.

A loss of spiritual orientation is quite normal during and after times of great stress. Habakkuk's cry to God expresses some of our own confusion and frustration as we try to interpret God's actions within the framework we are used to.

How long, O Lord, must I call for help,
but you do not listen?
Or cry out to you, 'Violence!'
but you do not save?
Why do you make me look at injustice?
Why do you tolerate wrong?
Destruction and violence are before me;
there is strife, and conflict abounds.
Therefore the law is paralysed,
and justice never prevails.
The wicked hem in the righteous,
so that justice is perverted.

(Habakkuk 1:2–4)

Job also lost all his familiar spiritual landmarks and
sank into confusion. He expresses his sense of disorienta-
tion in Job 9:22–24:

It is all the same; that is why I say,
'He destroys the blameless and the wicked.'
When a scourge brings sudden death,
He mocks the despair of the innocent.
When a land falls into the hands of the
    wicked,
He blindfolds its judges.
If it is not He, then who is it?

Often after a major traumatic event in our lives, we
need time to reflect and to rebuild lost confidence. The
loss of trust is what often distresses Christians. We want
to recapture a firm trust in God, but how do we do it? We
used to have a sense of reliance, a certain boldness in believing in God and His Word, but now we seem unable to
get a grip on Him again. We desperately need the biblical
sense of inner spiritual wholeness and well-being we once

enjoyed. Let us look at a few scriptural examples of the kind of healing that needs to take place in us.

> He heals the brokenhearted
> and binds up their wounds.
>
> (Psalm 147:3)

> Do not be wise in your own eyes;
> fear the Lord and shun evil.
> This will bring health to your body
> and nourishment to your bones.
>
> (Proverbs 3:7–8)

These two references speak of the inner sense of wholeness that comes to those who seek to walk in God's ways. 'Body' and 'bones' are sometimes used in Scripture to denote the whole person.

> Then your light will break forth like the dawn
> and your healing will quickly appear;
> then your righteousness will go
>   before you,
> and the glory of the Lord will be your
>   rear guard.
>
> (Isaiah 58:8)

God is promising renewed blessing to His people if they will forsake the emptiness of meaningless religious formalities for a true turning to Him. Alec Motyer says in his great commentary on Isaiah, 'The Prophecy of Isaiah', that this word 'healing' refers to personal restoration. He points out that the word 'ruka' is used in Jeremaiah 30:12 to describe new flesh growing over a wound and again in Nehemiah 4:1–2 to describe 'repair work'. Thus God promises to 'repair' his people, which is exactly what we need after we have faced tragedy. In Jeremiah 33:6–7 we read:

> 'Nevertheless, I will bring health and heal-
> ing to it; I will heal my people and will let
> them enjoy abundant peace and security . I
> will bring Judah and Israel back from captiv-
> ity and will rebuild them as they were be-
> fore.'

Like a flash of welcome light in an interminably dark tunnel comes this promise to an imprisoned Jeremiah. The prophet had consistently warned his people of their pend-ing defeat and captivity at the hands of the Babylonians. Now, typical of God who always stands by His servants in their darkest hour, comes a glimmer of hope. Healing means 'abundant peace and security'. That is what we lose in times of suffering and that is what needs to be restored. Derek Kidner draws our attention to the fact that our God 'reverses the reversal' ('The Message of Jeremiah', p. 114).

Here is a picture of the restoration we need. It is a healing of the inner person, a binding up of the wounds of the soul. It is an integration of the entire person; a restoration of the sense of peace and security that we once enjoyed. The question is: how does it happen?

Let us look at four areas of living that we need to take into account in the healing process.

Personality

You must remember that your personality and tem-perament are unique. You are not the same as anyone else and therefore the way you respond to the crises of life will be different from the way other people respond. We have certainly found this to be true in our own experience and we have observed this to be true in the lives of people we have dealt with over the years. It is the same what ever the crisis may be. People react differently although there may be certain common denominators.

For instance, in the loss of a loved one there is always grief, but the grief is not always expressed in the same way or for the same duration. Some people seem to be able to leap the hurdles with relative ease while others stumble and fall. You will have to take your own temperament and personality into account. It is important to be yourself and not to expect to keep pace with others. Let me remind you of God's gracious words to us concerning the way we are created:

> For you created my inmost being;
> you knit me together in my mother's womb.
> I praise you because I am fearfully and
> wonderfully made;
> your works are wonderful,
> I know that full well.
> My frame was not hidden from you
> when I was made in the secret place.
> When I was woven together in the
> depths of the earth,
> your eyes saw my unformed body.
> All the days ordained for me
> were written in your book
> before one of them came to be.
>
> (Psalms 139:13–16)

Notice that God creates our innermost being. The words 'my most inmost being' translate the Hebrew word 'reins' which refers to the most secret part of the human body, the inner nature. God created even that. Remem-

ber then that He created not only our physical body but
also the personality and temperament that go with it. Because we are all sinners, our personalities and temperaments need to be brought under the Lordship of Christ.
We cannot allow sinful facets of our personalities to remain unchecked. But taking that into account, we nevertheless need to thank God for who we are and act according to the way He has made us.

Our emotions are usually the area of our lives most
affected by suffering or tragedy. 'Uncertainty' is the word
that best describes those who have to cope with suffering.
I am aware that emotions are terribly complicated and
can often swing from one extreme to another. I am also
aware that often different feelings can overlap each other
during days of turmoil. However, I want to suggest that
there are basically three areas of our lives about which we
become most uncertain in times of stress.

Firstly, there is 'uncertainty about the future'. Anxiety sometimes overtakes us as we contemplate the consequences of what has happened. How will I live? Where
will the money come from? Will anyone marry me after a
rape? Where will I move to? How will I find a job? These
and a hundred other thoughts may plague us, depending
on our circumstances. We need to realise that anxiety and
concern about the future are normal for those facing tragic
loss. It is a time to reflect again on our Lord's words:

> Do not be afraid of those who kill the body
> but cannot kill the soul. Rather, be afraid of
> the One who can destroy both soul and body
> in hell. Are not two sparrows sold for a penny?
> Yet not one of them will fall to the ground
> apart from the will of your Father.
>
> (Matthew 10:28–29)

Secondly, there is sometimes 'uncertainty about the past'. Often guilt about things done long ago raises its ugly head when we are least able to cope with it. Arguments, harsh words, things done in secret long ago often come to haunt us in a moment of sadness and suffering.

Some years ago I visited a woman who was terminally ill with cancer. As the disease progressed and she grew weaker, she had only one cry on her lips, 'Will he forgive me, will he forgive me?' Sins of a dim and distant past paraded before her. Her husband had his own way of dealing with the crisis. He steadfastly refused to talk about it with her, or to let anyone else do so.

For Christians often the thought will arise that God is punishing us. As explained in the previous chapter, there are times when God's discipline occurs in our lives. But we must remember the fact that we live in a fallen world and are caught up in the natural tragedies of life. If we are Christians, we must resist the guilt that comes upon us from the past. As believers in Christ, we know that our sin and guilt has been dealt with on the cross. We must therefore lay hold of Paul's great statement in Romans 8:1 and truly believe it: 'Therefore, there is now no condemnation for those who are in Christ Jesus.'

But often 'uncertainty about the present' engulfs those caught up in sorrow and sadness. People with certain temperaments automatically assume that in some way they deserve what has happened to them. It may be conditioning from childhood or constant verbal abuse over the years that has stripped them of all sense of self-worth and dignity. They feel inferior, they believe that they are unable to cope, and they live with an ongoing sense of fear or dread. This maybe true even of Christians. They need to be encouraged to believe the promises in Scripture such as that contained in Hebrews 13:5–6

> 'Never will I leave you;
> never will I forsake you.'

So we say with confidence,

> 'The Lord is my helper; I will not be afraid.
> What can man do to me?'

All your own personality traits will be highlighted by the present events in your life. They may not all come to the fore immediately, but the different aspects of your personality will show as you grapple with the future, the past, and the present.

It is therefore important that you do not magnify your difficulties unnecessarily. There may be some personality types who will have to do great battle with themselves as they seek to cope with tragedy. If you are naturally melancholic, you may tend to brood and dwell on events and eventually sink into such a depth of self-pity that you will alienate your supportive friends and family. Other personalities naturally make a meal out of sorrow and engage in melodramatics which can also be off-putting. These things may need to be controlled. But remember that you are unique and you are permitted to be yourself. In seeking to rebuild your confidence, do not try to be somebody else. Deal with yourself as you are.

The will

I now turn to a second side of our nature that needs to be taken into account as we try to rebuild confidence, and that is the will. I am referring to that part of us that makes decisions about life; that hidden part of our total being where we instinctively evaluate the things we encounter in life—what different events mean to us; what we will do; what we will believe and how we will act. I suggest that three important decisions need to be made to assist us in the rebuilding process.

The first is a 'refusal to give in to discouragement'. It is impossible to banish all feelings of discouragement, but we do not need to be controlled by them. When some major suffering or tragedy has been experienced, quite often we experience an inability to function normally for a while. This in turn gives way to depression and discouragement. To be deprived of courage, confidence and the energy to do something positive can be severely debilitating. Although life may be very difficult for you while you are going through a period of mourning and grief, you need to remember that you are a Christian. There are certain things that are true of you. For instance, in Proverbs 24:16 we read:

> for though a righteous man falls seven
> times, he rises again.

A truly godly person may experience a number of setbacks in life. But the root of righteousness is in them. They belong to God. Not only will their view of life enable them to 'rise again', but so will the blessing and strength that God gives to his people in need. David experienced this confidence when he wrote:

> Though an army besiege me,
> my heart will not fear;
> though war break out against me,
> even then will I be confident.

> (Psalm 27:3)

A second decision of the will is to 'refuse to give into

self-pity'. This is a very subtle problem that often masquerades as the insensitivity of other people. We all have a basic love for ourselves that leads to self-centredness. In the Christian's life this is to be conquered so that we become other-people-centred. But in times of stress, when our guard is lowered and we are weaker than we would normally be, it is easy to give in to this enemy.

No one is immune to this danger. Even the great prophet Elijah seemed to experience a sense of self-pity when he ran for his life from Queen Jezebel and prayed that he might die. He thought that he was the only true prophet left in Israel and now they were seeking to kill him. God dealt wisely and gently with his exhausted and frightened servant. He gave him a time of rest and nourishment. Then he met with him and sent him right back into the battle, reminding him that he was not in fact the only one left but that there were 7000 others who had also remained true to God in spite of the pressure. The story is very movingly told in 1 Kings 19:1–18.

Most of the small quarrels and conflicts we have in life occur because self is being threatened, challenged or ignored. When something big happens, self can often become puffed up to enormous extremes. The problem is complicated because when the sorrow is great, people usually seek to be understanding and tolerant. But as Christians we must remember that we should display our faith in Christ even in our grief.

There is a third decision that needs to be made. The decision to begin to 'serve God again'.

Somebody once wrote 'Noble deeds and hot baths are the best cure for depression' (Penguin Dictionary of Modern Humorous Quotations, p. 73). This is a word of common sense to all.

There are two things we all need to do after times of unusual stress. The first is to find time to relax and reflect on what has happened, the 'hot baths' mentioned in the quote above. Reflection is very important. What has happened needs to be thought through. Unpleasantness needs to be faced. The whole experience has to be integrated into our view of God. We need to incorporate the experience into our lives.

The tragedy that overtook us at St James is a case in point. The event was so shocking and traumatic that it took some time for the reality to dawn on some people. It was an event so far outside our range of experience, so out of the ordinary, so totally unexpected, that the air of unreality was for many the first hurdle to cross. The days that followed were busy, traumatic and sad. The funeral services brought a finality that rounded off the event, but the funeral services could not provide the end point that some needed to reach. The event was bigger than the funeral. There were too many issues that needed to be thought through and the days between the attack and the funeral were too short. More time was necessary.

We were therefore very grateful for the very generous offer of holiday accommodation made by various people. We arranged to send a number of people away for a few days either to a quiet country hotel or a cottage at the sea. Here they had an opportunity to come to terms with what had happened.

But to avoid the pitfall of self-pity we need not only relaxation but also 'noble deeds'. In other words, as soon as you are able to, you ought to get involved in helping other people. Your focus should move to the needs of others. Go back to your Sunday School class or choir. Get back into the Bible study group. Start visiting those with ongoing needs. Offer your shoulder to someone else to cry on. Do not let your personal heartache cripple you spiritually. Remember that Jesus told us that the fields are ready for harvesting. He also said that some sow, some water, and some reap.

It is important to get back into circulation and enter the Lord's great field again—whether to plough, sow, water or reap. Not only is it important for you in terms of rebuilding your own life but it remains important in terms of your spiritual development. In all the difficulties of life we have the obligation to keep growing in the grace and the knowledge of our Lord.

There may be many other decisions to make as time goes by, but whatever your personal difficulty may be, these three things need to be kept before you—a refusal to give in to feelings of discouragement; a refusal to sink into self-pity, and a decision to get involved again in the work and witness of the gospel.

The understanding

The third area of our lives that we need to look at is the understanding. You need to confront what may be happening in your mind. Your thought life may be a jumble of confusion. Your thinking may swing from anger and bewilderment that God did not stop the event to attempts at explaining God's actions to sceptical friends and family. After a while your mind may settle into a perpetual state of doubt. This may add to your difficulty if you are a Christian because your honest questions and doubts may conflict with your belief that you ought to trust God whatever happens.

There are no ready-made answers for the individual struggles we have. As mentioned earlier, we all respond differently to crises. What may be a satisfactory answer to one is not necessarily a satisfactory answer to another. However I venture to make four suggestions for you to bear in mind as you seek to come to terms quickly with what is happening inside.

Firstly, 'don't try to justify God'. He needs no defence. We will save ourselves a lot of heartache if we can come to terms with the inscrutability of God. By this I mean that there is something about God's dealings with us that is mysterious and impenetrable. God does not always disclose to us the reasons why certain things happen. We often torture ourselves by asking the unanswerable 'why?' The truth is that we do not know why, and the sooner we come to terms with that the better. I do not mean to suggest that Christians should not do some heart-searching in the presence of God after a momentous event in their lives. There is always a need for inner reflection and evaluation. There are always lessons to learn. But I am referring to the unnecessary and ongoing torture that some people inflict on themselves in an attempt to penetrate the inscrutability of the divine will when it is utterly impossible. There is absolutely nothing wrong with replying to someone who asks, 'I simply don't know.'

We feel that if only we could arrive at some explanation or see some reason for the event, God would be protected from slander or ridicule. Believe me, God will survive! He is under no obligation to explain His actions to His creatures. There is however one thing of which we can be sure and that is that God is good. If He is good and yet permits evil things to happen in his world, we can only conclude that He has some ultimate good purpose and plan that He is working towards. The refuge we must finally shelter under is the Bible doctrine that the God and Father of our Lord Jesus Christ is *good*, even though at times He is inscrutable. Paul saw this and expressed it in this way:

> Oh, the depth of the riches of the
> wisdom and knowledge of God!
> How unsearchable His judgements,

and His paths beyond tracing out!
'Who has known the mind of the Lord?
Or who has been His counsellor?'
'Who has ever given to God,
that God should repay Him?'
For from Him and through Him and to
Him are all things.
To Him be the glory for ever! Amen.

(Romans 11:33–36)

How can we improve on such a statement? God's paths are beyond tracing out. Who has known the mind of the Lord? Yet to him, though mysterious and inscrutable, will be the glory for ever.

It took Job a little while to get to this point, but when he finally reached it, he said:

My ears had heard of you
but now my eyes have seen you.
Therefore I despise myself
and repent in dust and ashes.

(Job 42:5–6)

Thus the questions that trouble us now, the mystery of why whatever happened to us was permitted, the confusion and frustration of not seeing any immediate purpose or sense in it, all this will ultimately be swallowed up in the glory of God's presence. Don't try to justify God.

A second word of advice to those struggling with their thinking process is to remember to *distinguish between the emotional and the spiritual*. In more instances than I care to remember I have had to try to help people to see that their present feelings in a time of crisis are not a reflection of their status with God.

This is illustrated clearly in cases of marriage break-up. Often the betrayed and abandoned spouse concludes in her shock and sorrow that she must have done something wrong or else it would not have happened. So often I have had to point out the simple truth that men don't always need excuses to break up their homes. It was not necessarily the woman's fault. Her husband did what he wanted to do. It is as simple as that. In the same way, a cruel blow from life can leave us feeling so devastated that we come to wrong conclusions about ourselves. It is therefore important to draw very clear distinctions between the emotional upheaval you are going through and your relationship with your heavenly Father who is stable, unchanging and always loving.

Remember, Christians are still human. We also experience the sorrows and uncertainties of living in this world. We also grieve and weep as others do. And we also tend to make wrong judgements about ourselves when we are emotionally unstable. Your emotions may remain unstable for quite a while. You may even experience severe depression. But the one great unalterable fact is that you will always belong to Christ and he will always belong to you. Your sufferings do not change that, your emotional condition does not change that, and your circumstances can never change that great fact. Your spiritual status is fixed forever when you become a believer in the Lord Jesus Christ.

In the large evangelistic crusades conducted by Billy Graham some years ago, the famous gospel singer George Beverly Shea used to sing a song called 'Now I belong to Jesus':

> Jesus my Lord will love me forever
> From Him no pow'r of evil can sever;
> He gave His life to ransom my soul
> Now I belong to Him!

Now I belong to Jesus,
Jesus belongs to me
Not for the years of time alone,
But for eternity.

A third factor that needs to be borne in mind at this point is 'your physical condition'. It may be a small thing in your mind, but it is very important in assisting you to rebuild your confidence. During days of stress we tend not to eat. This is understandable but not advisable. It is particularly dangerous if, prior to the tragedy, you were ill and rundown. Tension and sorrow can rob us of vital calories and add immeasurably to a rundown condition. You therefore need to watch your physical condition and be careful not to develop unhealthy habits during your days of inner reconstruction. Proper food and rest are essential.

We were very grateful when a pharmaceutical company donated supplies of sleeping tablets to us in the aftermath of the attack on our church. They wisely foresaw the need to help people to sleep and not to remain sleepless because of stress. The tablets were very carefully made available by the medical doctor in charge of the debriefing process. In addition teams of monitors were set up to liaise with the bereaved and the injured. One of their functions was to provide meals for the families who had been severely traumatised or were too incapacitated to fend for themselves. We believe that these two simple functions of eating and sleeping helped people to recover sooner than they would have under other conditions.

A fourth important matter that needs to be mentioned for those trying to overcome the mental stress of a tragedy is to be aware of *the effect of other problems in your life*. Some people may have a host of problems with which they are struggling when they are suddenly caught up in a greater crisis. There may be a broken relationship or a strained family situation. It may be the loss of a job or a financial problem. The impact of the greater crisis has the effect of heightening the previous troubles. All your problems now become jumbled up and one set of answers does not satisfy everything. Anxiety is deepened and it is difficult to see through the confusion. The truth is that you may be struggling with more than one problem. Not only do you have to deal with the crisis on hand but you also have other unresolved difficulties with which to cope.

For instance, a young girl who has been sexually molested by her father carries a great burden with which she needs help. If she suffers the misfortune of being raped by someone else, for example a boyfriend, she now has two different problems to handle although they may be confused and merged in her own mind. She has been betrayed and abused by two different people under different circumstances. If she later suffers the further tragedy of the loss of a young child through illness or accident and the two previous problems of molestation and rape have not been resolved, she adds yet a third problem to the burden she carries.

In our own case there were those injured or traumatised who were struggling with other great personal difficulties. For a while all the problems seemed merged into one great burden. These people needed help to see that there were often several different issues that needed attention. When they understood this and were able to separate the issues in their minds, anxiety lessened and each problem became more manageable.

Remember that in the process of rebuilding your confidence, you need to face the tensions you carry in your mind. One way of doing this is to be aware of the possibility of one problem intruding on another thereby creating confusion and increased anxiety.

Your spiritual life

During a time of crisis all areas of our lives need attention but none as urgently as our walk with God. The fourth area of the spiritual life is the essential dimension to healing and wholeness.

The temptation to succumb spiritually is very great during the awful days of confusion and anger that often follow a crisis. Sometimes we have no one else to vent our feelings on but God. The great struggle between faith and the natural desire for answers and clarification can take the form of spiritual sulking. We don't talk to God. We often won't talk to Him. We feel helpless and disadvantaged . He has all the power, He knows what is going on, but we are in the dark. So we lapse into a spiritual limbo, a no-man's-land where feelings are numbed and nothing appears to be real anymore. While this is understandable, we must guard against it. We are not called on to be what we are not, but we are called to be what we are—Christians.

There are certain fundamental principles that we need to remember to help us maintain our spiritual equilibrium during troubled days.

First, *live for eternity*. Bear in mind the great truth that this world is not our final home. We are being prepared for a new world, free of the trouble and woe that plague us here. This is not escapism, nor is it an invitation to withdraw from this world and its sorrows. Rather, it puts meaning into all we do here. Christians should not hold too tightly to the world and material possessions. We can ultimately keep none of these. We will use them while we need to live in this world and where possible to help others less fortunate than ourselves, but we will not anchor ourselves to possessions.

When we live for eternity we live with the reminder

that life on earth is uncertain. It is not pessimistic but realistic to recognise that there is really nothing we can count on in this life. We cannot depend on health for it may break down at any time. We can enjoy it while we have it and we can even seek to extend it, but we cannot count on it. The same applies to money which is here today and gone tomorrow. Sadly, the same is true of friends. We may have many good friends of long-standing but we know that while some will stand by us through thick and thin, not all will. Many have been disappointed by friends and family who they thought loved them and valued them. The jobs we choose, the fame we achieve— all may be gone in a moment. Except for a few die-hard fans who remember the names of the great sport stars, movie stars or politicians of yesteryear, these once-famous people end up as a name in a history book or a wax model in a museum somewhere for a little while.

We need to take the long view. We need to remember that we will never die. God, the only immortal Being, has granted our souls an immortality that will last forever. We are creatures of eternity and all the events that overtake us in time ought to be evaluated in the light of eternity.

Secondly, we must bear in mind *the coming Day of Judgement*. The unfair and unjust event that overtook you is one of a long history of such events in this world. There are simply too many atrocities in the history of our world for there to be no Day of Judgement. The criminals who shot our congregation; the hit-and-run driver who killed that husband, father or child; the man or woman who breaks up a family, the swindler who gets away with his crime must be made to answer. There must be a Day of Judgement. It is all we have. It is the only thing that enables us to face life with any certainty. Those who deny such a day of accounting are really saying that justice does not matter. If that is so, then nothing ever matters again.

But it is not so. Things do matter. Justice must be done and be seen to be done.

Much of the violence in South Africa has been so horrific that it almost defies description. The aggravating factor is that the perpetrators are seldom caught. On the rare occasions that they are caught, we have been treated to the spectacle of demonstrations for their release. It is as if what they did either did not matter or is excusable or justifiable politically. But as Christians we remember that there is a Judge of all the earth before whom we all stand. No one will ultimately get away.

That is what gave our church members the courage and confidence after the attack, and confounded the media. We did not want personal revenge. We wanted the law to take its course and the criminals to be brought to book. But we knew that ultimately they would stand before Him to whom the whole earth is accountable. Paul stated it clearly in Acts 17:31:

> For He has set a day when He will judge the
> world with justice by the man He has ap-
> pointed. He has given proof of this to all men
> by raising Him from the dead.

The perplexed and troubled writer of Psalm 73 came to a place of peace and rest in his own mind when he understood the final destiny of the world:

> When I tried to understand all this,
> it was oppressive to me
> till I entered the sanctuary of God;
> then I understood their final destiny.
> Surely you place them on slippery ground;
> you cast them down to ruin.
> How suddenly are they destroyed,
> completely swept away by terrors!

As a dream when one awakes,
so when you arise, O Lord,
you will despise them as fantasies.

(Psalm 73:16–20)

Thirdly, to retain your grip on God during days of trial make sure, as suggested earlier, that you *continue to make spiritual progress*. Do not stay on the outskirts of the life of your church. Some people are content to sit in the back seats of the church and observe what is going on without participating in the life of the church. Resist that tendency. It will be especially strong during a time of sorrow or grief. You may feel that you desire no deep involvement. Indeed it may be expedient for you to withdraw for a while. But there must be a return to active fellowship. If you are not a member of a church, make up your mind to become one. Do not be static—make progress spiritually. Be determined to grow inwardly, to learn all you can about the Bible, and to serve others in the cause of the kingdom of God.

A fourth consideration to help you spiritually is to determine to *put right the things that are wrong*.

The night of our tragedy was a night of a rapid shifting of priorities. Suddenly life seemed so fleeting. The petty things that keep us apart from each other were shown up for what they are—pettiness, silliness, childishness and immaturity. Family relationships became important. Friends became important. Everything was thrown into sharp focus. You may have gone through something similar.

Take the opportunity of restoring broken relationships. Make whatever apologies are necessary. Be willing to eat humble pie and don't be caught up in the pettiness of who said what and when and who was wrong or right. I have often made the observation that five minutes before

I die, it will not matter one whit to me who won the last argument. I will have other things of far greater importance on my mind. Let them be on my mind now. Let's be done with the unimportant things. Place a new and greater value on family and friends. Do the good you have been waiting to do but never got around to doing. Give away the money you intended to give, write that letter you have been putting off, give that word of thanks and encouragement. Draw up a will if you have not done so.

Above all, make sure that your walk with God is sincere, real and biblical. We encouraged the survivors at our church to see their lives as a second chance to live for God, to do good and get involved. Most importantly, we have stressed that if they have not yet done so and have survived a tragedy, that it is a second chance to turn to Christ and become a Christian. Many have done so. Have you ?

6

Learning to Pray Again

In the aftermath of the horror that descended on our church the night the terrorists struck, Christians en countered two puzzling reactions within themselves. On the one hand they had an unusual sense of the presence of God. In the midst of grief and shock, people had an almost inexpressible awareness that they were being held in a mighty unseen grip, steadying them and supporting them. Their consciousness of God and of the privilege of belonging to him was greatly heightened during the dark days of sorrow that followed. But on the other hand almost all who were affected by the massacre found themselves unable to commune with God as they used to do. Time and again during debriefing sessions, in personal conversations and in prayer meetings people referred to this difficulty.

Quite understandably this is an additional stress factor for Christians because prayer and communion with our heavenly Father is our very lifeblood. It is the air we breathe. Yet in spite of years of faithful Christian living, a true faith in Jesus Christ and an ongoing conviction that God had not deserted them, Christians reported a new dimension of struggle in the realm of prayer.

This difficulty in prayer is often seen in the aftermath of the personal tragedies that people experience. Even if the tragedy occurred before the person became a Christian, it is possible for the after effects to play havoc with their Christian lives. A woman wrote a long and moving letter to my wife describing how, as a teenager, she was raped by a family friend. Much has been written about rape and its victims in recent times, so it will be no surprise to learn that one of the after effects for this young girl was the awful feeling of being physically dirty and contaminated.

In her case the rape was particularly cruel and vile. The needless and irrational cruelty that so often accompanies sexual crime is one of the evidences of the sinfulness of the human heart. It was so in her case. The leering laughter of her attacker as he fled, leaving her bound, violated and semiconscious, haunted her for years. She washed and bathed compulsively and often had bouts of vomiting in an attempt to erase the feelings of defilement she carried deep within. She finally met the man of her dreams and married him. He was every inch a gentleman and his patience and gentleness carried her through the difficulties of the early years of their marriage. Those years were a sexual nightmare as she constantly relived her terrible ordeal. After an attempt at sex, she would flee to the bathroom to vomit.

After the woman and her husband both found Christ, things improved greatly. Then another tragedy struck. She was unable to conceive. Quite naturally she associated this with the sordidness of the crime perpetrated against her. Like so many people who have suffered trauma and tragedy, she felt that God was somehow against her. Although she was now a believer in Jesus, her spiritual struggles took on a new dimension.

Then one wonderful night in a special meeting in the church, the entire body of believers prayed for her. In a quiet and simple act of fellowship, the preacher placed his hands on her head and asked God to be pleased to touch his dear wounded and hurting child in a special way. Somehow that night a new sense of hope was born and that very night she conceived the first of her four children.

Our walk with God

The point I want to make is how deeply violence and tragedy can affect our walk with God. In her letter to my wife, this woman wrote:

> After I became a Christian I still used to feel self-doubt. Satan used the rape as a means of keeping me down in depression and constantly unsure of myself as a Christian. But I used to carry a picture of Christ on the cross around with me. One day it dawned on me that he too was betrayed by a friend. Then I thought of how degraded he must have felt hanging naked on a cross. This thought has lodged itself deep in my heart. I often reflect on it when I am feeling low or morbid. I thought of that little word 'so' in John 3:16, and put my name into the space where 'the world' should be: 'For God *so* loved *me* that He gave his one and only Son'. Slowly I began to heal inside and to recover my confidence in God and to see that I was normal after all.

So many people go through a spiritual wilderness after a tragedy. We have seen that tragedy means different things to different people but almost without exception, people testify to a sense of uncertainty in the presence of God; they do not know how to pray; they often experience a loss of concentration in reading their Bibles, in church or in the act of prayer. I am aware that these are problems with which all Christians struggle in the normal course of life but after trials or suffering, we often experience an added difficulty in our walk with God. Let us look more closely at several of these areas.

Uncertainty and doubt

Our doubts about God may take several forms. Firstly, we may feel uncertain about our relationship with him. In our case a number of people reported feeling that in some way God was especially angry with them. They could not rationalise their feelings except to say that they felt guilty before God. They felt helpless, wondering what they had done wrong.

Do you feel like that? If you have suffered some sadness in your life, it is quite possible that you may experience a sense of abandonment, a feeling that God has left you. You may feel isolated and terribly alone. Although this is an understandable reaction, you must remember that it is not true.

Secondly, an uncertainty about God may show itself in a secret doubt about whether what we have always believed is true. It is like being betrayed by a friend you have always trusted and defended. Suddenly you are confused and do not know what to say. You may have doubts about the validity of the gospel and its relevance in our world. The problem is that these feelings often clash with the long-standing clearly defined convictions we have had about God, His goodness and His promises. We find ourselves entering silent but enormous battles. We bravely try to keep up our devotional habits as Christians, but the secret doubts and hurts eat away at us.

Concentration

Yet another struggle is the battle to concentrate. We

read the Bible but cannot remember what we have read from one verse to the next. To concentrate in prayer is a battle anyway but now we may find it almost impossible. We try to pray but our words or thoughts drift off into all sorts of highways and byways. A thousand different issues fly through our minds and we brood over the sad events in our lives. It is not easy to forget and we cannot simply banish things to the back of our minds.

God's presence

For Christians the apparent loss of a sense of God's presence is often the most distressing aspect of suffering. In this book I want to testify to the wonderful sense of God's presence with us in our time of sorrow. But there are times in the midst of our suffering when God just does not seem to be there. We wish we could feel him or sense that he is there. We feel we need tangible proof of His presence but it seems to us that the heavens are made of brass and there is no one up there who loves us or listens to us.

Yet we must remember we have lost nothing of God. Our feelings do not tell the whole story. He is with us in all our hurt. We are His children and He is fully aware of what we are experiencing. He who sent His Son to die for us will surely give us all things in Christ . If He has done the greatest thing for us in sending Christ to the cross, is He incapable of doing the lesser things for us, in keeping us in the midst of life's trials? No, the apostle Paul says emphatically. In all those things we are more than conquerors. He goes on to make this great statement about Christians and their God in the midst of all the upheavals of life:

> For I am convinced that neither death nor
> life, neither angels nor demons, neither the
> present nor the future, nor any powers, nei-
> ther height nor depth, nor anything else in
> all creation, will be able to separate us from
> the love of God that is in Christ Jesus our
> Lord.
>
> (Romans 8:38–39)

Whatever we may feel as hurt and damaged emotions
surge within our breast, the fact is that we are not sepa-
rated from the love of God that is in Jesus Christ our
Lord.

Faith

It is at this point that the struggle of faith takes place.
Often we have been told that faith is our ability to pray
through to a great emotional sense of victory. Or else it is
the tenacious ability to so prevail with God that we force
his arm either to heal our illnesses or to reverse our mis-
fortunes. But this is a misrepresentation of the struggle of
faith. Faith, to put it simply, is the conviction that God
does not tell lies.

Faith understands that, though we live in this world
and are often caught up in suffering and tragedy, the Good
Shepherd is still with His sheep. He does not leave them
to be swallowed up by the ravenous forces of this world.
Faith understands that the love of God in Jesus Christ for
His people is something that is settled for ever. It is unchanging and unchangeable. It is rooted in the mysterious eternal purpose of God, demonstrated by Christ dying on the cross and displayed for us by the gracious way
He called us to Himself even though we were unwilling

rebels. His love for us is not something which is affected by what we do or don't do. Nor is it dependent on how we feel from day to day. It is entirely unconditional on His part. However unlovable we may have been in the past, the wonder is that He still loves us.

As you battle with the raging forces within you, as your own feelings or sense of awareness of God ebbs and flows in the aftermath of some experience of suffering, you need to exercise *faith* in the truth of His love for you. Faith and feelings so often clash in the heart of the believer. But faith refuses to allow feelings to call the shots. Faith insists that what is ultimately true is what God has said in His Word and not what my heart is saying because of sorrow, shock or depression.

The woman referred to above added several words to the bottom of the last page of her letter. She was trying to express the fierce emotional battle she endured for years and in large letters summarised the struggle in the following words:

- struggle to understand
- suicidal
- empty vacuum
- confusion
- withdrawal
- anger
- hurt
- rebellion
- acceptance
- bitterness
- virgin

These last two words described the heartache she endured at losing her virginity in such a brutal way. She did not automatically lose all these problems when she became a Christian. Nor did she win any of these emotional battles overnight. It was a slow process of taking one step at a time. She learned to trust God and finally her faith won the day.

I have taken some time to discuss the emotional turmoil that often follows a tragedy because it is important to know that the feelings with which we struggle are normal. When we are trying to re-establish our relationship with God, we sometimes feel that no one else is having these battles. But this is not true. Many of our struggles are common to all. How then do we pick up the pieces and learn to pray again?

The way back

Because of the tendency we all have to become oversensitive and even irrational in our assessments of ourselves, it is important to 'exercise common sense'. As I have just said, one thing to remember is that you are not the only one suffering in this way. You must avoid the trap of feeling that your sufferings are unique. If you want to start praying again, begin by telling God that you know that many of His children have had to endure severe trials. Tell Him that you believe that as He has been with them, he will also be with you.

Secondly, learn to *face your trauma honestly*. Why do I say this? It is possible to be emotionally dishonest with ourselves and so to complicate our problems. When the disaster overtook our church, the enormity of what happened was too much for Bill. He simply switched off. He refused to acknowledge the event. It was not that he denied the actual happening but rather he refused to allow his emotions to deal with it. He seemed to sail through the tragedy unaffected. Six weeks later he sank into an inexplicable depression.

Conversely, we saw some manifestations of melodrama as people used the event for manipulative purposes—either to gain attention or to resurrect some imagined illness. One lady actually used the massacre as an argument in court to get out of paying a traffic fine saying she was distraught because of what had happened. She was not even in the church at the time of the attack!

The way back to a regular walk with God is to face up honestly and sensibly to what happened in your life. You may need a friend or a counsellor to help you to understand your feelings. Then you need to take those true feelings into the presence of the Lord in prayer and honestly talk to Him about them. The wonderful thing about being God's child is that there are no secrets between Him and us . He knows all things. We may freely confess to him all our fear, anger, shock, disappointment, confusion and hurt.

I often think of our Lord's meeting with the apostle Peter after the resurrection. You will remember how Peter denied Christ three times on the night of his crucifixion although Peter made loud affirmations of his loyalty to Christ even to death (John 13:37). Then came that memorable meeting between Jesus and Peter on the seashore. Jesus asked Peter twice 'Do you truly love me?' (John 21:15, 1 6).

Can you imagine how Peter felt? How would you have felt if, after promising to stay with Jesus to the death, you denied him three times? I can only begin to imagine the humiliation, regret, remorse and self-loathing in Peter's heart. I must pause at this point to say that it is indeed possible for someone who truly loves Christ to 'deny' him momentarily in a time of fear and upheaval. To love Christ and yet to behave in a way that denies our love for him is sadly all too often the experience of the Christian believer. This is because we struggle constantly with sinful natures that have to cope with the changing pressure brought upon us by a fallen world. Yet I want you to notice what Peter did. He said twice: 'Yes, Lord, you know that I love you.' Then, on the third occasion, he said: 'Lord, you know all things; you know that I love you' (John 21:17).

When Peter could point to no external evidence of his love for Christ, he appealed to Christ's omniscience. 'Lord, you know all things.' What an encouragement this is to us. Surely all Christians should learn how to relate to the attributes of God in their daily walk with Him. What Peter was saying in effect was: 'Lord, you know that I boasted that I would stand by you even if it meant death. You know that I failed miserably. You know my inner agony of spirit, my sense of unworthiness, my fear and confusion. But Lord, you also know about my bitter tears of remorse and repentance, my deep regrets and, above all, that in spite of my failure on the night, deep in my heart I do really love you. What else can I appeal to, Lord? My shame is great. I have no way of proving to you how I feel. Therefore I appeal to your deity, your omniscience. Here is my heart—probe it and search it. Lord, you know I love you.'

This is a lovely and long neglected aspect of prayer for all who are trying to pick up pieces. Why don't you try it? Be honest about your feelings—not only in terms of your loss or hurt, but also in terms of how you feel about God. Lay bare your heart to Him. Take your doubt and depression to Him and say to Him: 'Lord, you know all things. You know that I love you.'

The third thing to bear in mind as we re-establish our personal communion with God is that we need to 'submit to His will for us'. In other words, we must be content to let God be God. We can do nothing about our circumstances. What is done is done. We do not always know the reason, therefore we must acknowledge that God's plans are inscrutable. His judgements are unsearchable and his paths beyond tracing out (Romans 11:33).

As long as we harbour feelings that God has to explain Himself to us, we will live with bitterness and resentment against Him. He simply will not always explain Himself to us and He certainly is not answerable to us. As we take up again the position of a disciple sitting at His feet, we must be content to leave the unanswered questions with Him and submit to his dealings with us.

Because we do not know why the event happened, we must focus on what we do know. We know that God is good and that he loves us. He has promised that He works all things for good for those who love Him and are called according to his purpose (Romans 8:28). Do we believe this? Will faith rise to the occasion and say 'I believe this', or will we go on chafing inside and lose all sense of peace?

As we surrender daily to God and His will for us, an increasing sense of peace and spiritual equilibrium will return.

Let us turn now to the actual problem of engaging in prayer.

The problem of prayer

It seems to me that the problem of prayer is often approached from the wrong direction. So often we concentrate on methods to help us in our prayer times. As a fellow struggler in this area, I want to pay tribute to all those fine Christian friends and preachers who have helped me over the years to keep in touch with God through prayer. I have experimented with various methods and systems to make my own personal devotions more meaningful and indeed some of them have done so. All of us need to have a system. If we do not find an orderly way to approach God, we will always struggle in our Christian

faith. But over the years I have become convinced that
the need to discover a method that works for us is not our
primary need, nor is it the primary problem in prayer. Let
us look at Romans 8:26–27:

> In the same way, the Spirit helps us in our
> weakness. We do not know what we ought
> to pray for, but the Spirit Himself intercedes
> for us with groans that words cannot express.
> And He who searches our hearts knows the
> mind of the Spirit, because the Spirit inter-
> cedes for the saints in accordance with God's
> will.

We are told that our primary problem in prayer is not
how to pray but rather *what* to pray. When I first began to
understand this concept, I really struggled with it. But as
I allowed the matter to settle in my mind and heart over a
period of time, I slowly came to understand that *what* to
say to God is exactly my problem in prayer.

How often have you not gone into the presence of
God to pray with a heart full of feelings, thoughts and
longings, but been unable to articulate them in such a
way that you feel you have really prayed. You may have
gone to pray with a most sincere desire to meet with God
only to find all your thoughts jumbled and your words
dammed up. Sometimes the feelings we experience seem
to defy human language. When we try to express our
thoughts our words seem puerile and totally inadequate
to describe what is happening in our hearts . Why do we
feel like this? To answer the question we need to take a
step back. Let's go back to the beginning of Romans 8:26.

We need to note two factors as we struggle to learn
again how to pray. The first of these is described as 'our
weakness'.

Our weakness

What is this weakness? Many biblical scholars believe it refers to an area that may be plaguing us at any given time. Thus it refers to the specific sense of weakness we all experience when we come to pray. However most commentators would agree that it could have a different application. It could in fact be a reference to the general state of spiritual weakness in which the human race finds itself because of our fallen condition.

Sin has affected everything. Before our first parents sinned against God in Eden, there was no weakness in his magnificent creation. But after that devastating act of disobedience, everything changed. Death and weakness obtained a foothold and worked their destruction in every facet of our being. The wonder of the communion with God which Adam and Eve enjoyed on a regular basis was broken. Enmity and alienation were introduced. The condition of people today is such that they do not naturally seek God but rather oppose him and rebel against him.

When we become Christians our relationship with God is restored. This is a wonderful consequence of God's grace extended to us in Jesus Christ. Our sins are forgiven and we are adopted into his worldwide family. However, glorious as this act is, it does not automatically cancel out the weakness and frailty of our human nature. We bring our previous frailties into the Christian life and we slowly learn to deal with them as we grow in grace. But all the changes that need to be effected in us are not made overnight.

Our weakness as sinful human beings, albeit saved through Christ, can be displayed in a number of ways. For instance it may take a while for some people to overcome the bad habits that have accrued over the years. Things like excessive drinking, smoking or bad language don't always drop off immediately although there are occasions when they do. Some Christians may have been enslaved to pornography in their pre-conversion days and may find that this destructive habit is a constant battleground in their new life. Others struggle with previously uncontrolled tempers and unkind speaking habits.

All these and a myriad other things are demonstrations that we are 'weak'. But without a doubt the area where our weakness is felt the keenest is in the area of prayer. When we come on our knees before the One who inhabits eternity, the great and holy God, the Father of our Lord Jesus Christ, it often seems as if our tongues are tied and the profound feelings and thoughts that stir in our breast are destined never to be expressed.

If this is the experience of all Christians to at least some extent, what happens when the burden of tragedy and suffering is added to our weakness? Prayer is a struggle under normal circumstances, but what about abnormal circumstances? When we struggle with utter confusion at God's ways, the hurt and bewilderment of loss or injury, how do we deal with the awful feeling that maybe, just maybe, God is not listening to us?

The good news is that Romans 8:26–27 introduces another factor into the troublesome matter of prayer and our relationship with God: the Holy Spirit.

The Holy Spirit

There is so much to know about the Holy Spirit, the wonderful third Person in the holy Trinity. I simply want to point out in this section how He helps us in the matter of prayer.

You may be familiar with the story of Mary and Martha and the dinner party they organised for Jesus (Luke 10:38–

42). Martha felt harassed by all the preparations needed to feed her household guests. Mary, on the other hand, abandoned the kitchen in favour of sitting at Jesus' feet. She felt it was more important to be fed by Him than for Him to be fed by her. Martha, feeling a little annoyed at being left to carry the responsibilities, came to Jesus and said: 'Lord, don't you care that my sister has left me to do the work by myself? Tell her to help me!'

Did you know that this is the only place in the New Testament, apart from Romans 8:26, where this word 'help' is used? I am sure the Holy Spirit ensured it was recorded in this way so that we would understand the help He gives us in prayer. What Martha was requesting was that Mary would come and 'pick up her end of the burden'. That is what this lovely word means. It refers to that act whereby somebody comes alongside you and helps you to shoulder the burden you are carrying. That is exactly what the Holy Spirit does in the matter of prayer. He helps us in our weakness or, if you like, He comes alongside us as we seek God's face in prayer and takes up one end of the burden.

When we pray to our Father in heaven He does not leave us to struggle on by ourselves. He has sent His Spirit to live in us and to be with us. One way in which the Spirit demonstrates that He is with us is by assisting us in our communion with God.

This is a real encouragement for those who are struggling with re-establishing their prayer times after a traumatic experience. You do not need to fret about prayer or to get hot and bothered because you can't feel the presence of God. Your feelings of numbness and inability to concentrate are well understood by your Father. Yet your prayers are still heard, for there is an unseen Presence standing with you and assisting you as you pray.

But how does He help us? In what way do we benefit

from His presence? After all, the struggle is still ours. We still need some assurance that we are making contact with headquarters again.

Inexpressible groans

The phrase 'groans that words cannot express' has been the source of much debate by various Bible commentators. William Hendricksen believes that in some wonderful though indefinable way the Holy Spirit himself groans on our behalf and so intercedes for us in our troubles and trials. If Christ could intercede for us as indicated in Romans 8:34, is it not possible for the Spirit to do so too? This is a very plausible and attractive interpretation of the phrase which would highlight the wonderful role the Holy Spirit plays in the life of a Christian. He is after all our Helper. Whatever merit this opinion has, I think the better explanation of this difficult phrase is given by the early 19th century biblical scholar Robert Haldane:

> Although these sighings or groanings of the children of God are here ascribed to the Holy Spirit, it is not to be supposed that the Divine Spirit can be subject to such emotions or perturbations of mind; but it is so represented, because He draws forth these groans from our hearts and excites them there. Thus it is *our* hearts that groan, but the operation and emotion is from the Holy Spirit; for the subject of these, and He who produces them, must not be confounded.
>
> (An Exposition of the Epistle of the Romans, p. 387)

In other words the Holy Spirit is not the one who is actually doing the groaning; we are. Why should the third Person of the Trinity groan? Groaning implies perplexity and unhappiness. He is not perplexed or unhappy. He is divine and knows all things. He knows the will of God. But we do not. We struggle with our burden of weakness. We are perplexed. We often do not know what course of action to take, what decision to make, or how to interpret events that overtake us. Moreover, when we try to pray, our weakness and ignorance seem to overrule us so that we do not know what to say to God. But thank God He has not left us helpless to bear our burdens alone. He has sent His Holy Spirit to help us, to take His end of the task.

The Holy Spirit does this in the matter of prayer. He puts thoughts into our minds, prompts us as to what we should say. He stirs up within our hearts longings, yearnings and sighs and He gives them validity. He empowers our poor petitions. The best way to capture the tension we experience between how we feel and our inability to express it is the word 'groan'. Thus you should not be discouraged by your seeming inability to pray. Our heavenly Father knows what you need. He knows what you are saying. The Holy Spirit adds an empowerment even to the half-expressed thoughts, words and sighs of our spirit.

> The people of God are often so much oppressed, and experience such anguish of mind, that their agitated spirits, borne down by affliction, can neither perfectly conceive nor properly express their complaints and request to God. Shall they then remain without prayer? No; the Holy Spirit acts in their hearts, exciting in them sighs and groans. Such appear to have been the groanings of Hezekiah, when he said, 'Like a crane or a swallow, so did I

chatter; I did mourn as a dove; mine eyes fail with looking upward; O Lord, I am oppressed, undertake for me.' Such also was the experience of David in the seventy-seventh Psalm, when he says, 'I am so troubled that I cannot speak.' Thus, too, Hannah 'spake in her heart; only her lips moved, but her voice was not heard.' No words of Peter in his repentance are recorded; his groanings are represented by his weeping bitterly; and in the same way we read of the woman who was a sinner as only washing the feet of Jesus with her tears, which expressed the inward groanings of her heart. (Ibid p. 388)

Thus the experience of God's children under trial is often so deep that they have no words to pray. How wonderful to remember that our God is a Trinity; Father, Son and Holy Spirit are all engaged in helping us in the matter of prayer and communion.

Two intercessors

Christians are described as having two intercessors. In Romans 8:26 it is the Holy Spirit who intercedes. But in verse 34 Christ Jesus is at the right hand of God interceding for us. What an enormous privilege for beleaguered Christians struggling with tragedy.

In what way can it be said that both the Spirit and Christ intercede for us? Perhaps the easiest way to illustrate this is to draw the analogy of appearing in a law court. When our advocate has to address the court on our behalf and plead our innocence, he illustrates what Jesus does for us at the right hand of God. He presents His atoning sacrifice as a constant reminder that our penalty has been paid and our sins have been forgiven. We are justified and need no longer fear the judgement of God.

But when we have to stand up and address the court ourselves to plead our case, our advocate needs to advise us what to say. This can be said to illustrate the role the Holy Spirit plays in the prayer life of the Christian. He teaches us what to say and makes our inarticulate longings perfectly intelligible to God. When we need someone to plead for us, we turn to our great Substitute who died on the cross and rose again. When we need to touch the throne of grace to receive help in a time of trouble, we call on our great Comforter to help us with the groanings of our heart.

A word of caution needs to be sounded. We must never fall into the trap of thinking that the Holy Spirit does it all while we sit back and relax. No, we are called on to pray. It is our prayer, our sighs, our groans with which He works. The power is His but the groans are ours. We must still be constantly at the work of prayer, seeking the face of God. As we do so, we find that He draws near to us and takes up His side of the task and helps us. Thank God that He does.

According to his will

What do we say to a bereaved person whose loved one was killed in a violent crime; the person whose life is cut short by a terminal illness; the rape victim who constantly washes herself to get rid of the feeling of filth? Can they continue praying even when their minds are bereft of words and they can hardly formulate thoughts? The answer is yes! Don't stop praying. Don't be discouraged. Keep on, even if it is only sighs and groans that you can present to God, because we are assured that God hears them. Read Romans 8:27 again:

> And he who searches our hearts knows the mind of the Spirit, because the Spirit intercedes for the saints in accordance with God's will.

We are told that the God knows our hearts. It is a reminder of the great words of Jeremiah 17:10:

> I the Lord search the heart
> and examine the mind,
> to reward a man according to his conduct,
> according to what his deeds deserve.

God knows what is going on inside and He understands what we are trying to say because he 'knows the mind of the Spirit' who is helping us, prompting us and drawing groans from us to present to Him. All our wishes, longings, prayers, aspirations, ideas, and burdens are plain to him.

Sometimes Christians have longings that the world would never understand. Our values are different to those of the world. We grieve over things that don't affect the world. If somebody dies without knowing Christ as Saviour, it adds a dimension of sorrow to our grief that the world would find hard to comprehend. But God knows.

He understands even the faintest flicker of the hearts of His children suffering tragedy in this world. He welcomes our groans and sighs. He does not accuse us of prayerlessness or spiritual fickleness. He tenderly gathers our longings into the embrace of His will and draws near to us in our sorrow.

Even more wonderful is that we have the assurance

that when we cry to Him in this way, it is 'in accordance with God's will'. The Holy Spirit would never help us with prayers and petitions that are outside the will of God. The Spirit takes up our burden with us be cause God has sent Him to do so.

God's comfort

God knew that we would struggle in this world with all its pressures. He knows that we are weak and that we often live with perplexity and confusion. So part of His plan for us was to send the Holy Spirit. Not only does he help us in our prayers but He lives inside all God's children. Because of the presence of the Holy Spirit within us, we are able to persevere in a world of difficulty, in the face of suffering. It is the fulfilment of the promise of Jesus to His disciples on the night before His death when he said:

> I will ask the Father, and he will give you another Counsellor to be with you for ever—the Spirit of truth. The world cannot accept him, because it neither sees him nor knows him. But you know him, for he lives with you and will be in you. I will not leave you as orphans; I will come to you.
>
> (John 14:16–18)

This leads me to comment on the three little words in Romans 8:27 'for the saints'. All these blessings, all this help in prayer, is for Christians only. This is part of the experience and privilege given to the people of God. It is true that Christians often suffer and weep. Yes, they may experience tragedy and tears. They may also be the victims of injustice, persecution or criminal activity. But the other side of the story is that they have the Holy Spirit. His divine power and help is theirs and theirs alone.

I know that Christians are not the only people who pray. Prayer is endemic to the human race which is, as we know, incurably religious us. But non-Christians know nothing of the privilege about which we are speaking here. For Christians there is none of the fear that drives others to seek their deity. We do not sit mutely before an impersonal fate that needs to be warded off with hopeless rituals. Rather, we are in the hands of a loving Father who understands our bewilderment and has provided for us to maintain or to re-establish our communion with him when life becomes too much.

We need to take heart. We are not alone. As Jesus promised, He has not left us as orphans. He is with us through the presence of the Holy Spirit. It may not be easy to learn to pray again. We may sometimes feel we are not making much progress, but we are not always the best judges of our spiritual progress. It is enough that we have His promise. We are His, and He is ours. He has not left us or forsaken us.

Even in the face of life's tragedies we can truthfully say He loves us. We may bring our aching, breaking hearts to Him. We may bring our sighs and groans to Him and be assured that He hears us and knows what we are trying to say. He approves of our prayers and accepts them. And we may confidently look for Him to answer in due time because our groans are 'in accordance with God's will'.

7

Forgiveness

We now approach a subject of great sensitivity and one filled with great complexities. The question of forgiveness must be faced if we are to overcome the devastation of tragedy and suffering. Of course not all suffering is caused by another person. Natural disasters, freak accidents and debilitating sickness are not the fault of another human being. In such cases anger and confusion may be the issue rather than forgiveness. But all too often we are the victims of the criminal activity or the negligence of others. In these cases our sense of outrage and justice may simply not be satisfied by the due process of law. Either the offender gets away with his crime or the sentence is so lenient that it only serves to strengthen our sense of anger and injustice.

A good illustration of this occurred some years ago in Cape Town. A youth group from one of the group of churches for which I am responsible went on a Friday night outing to an ice skating rink. They used a number of vehicles to transport the youth. When they returned home, one vehicle remained behind to pick up the dawdlers. It was driven by my 35-year-old cousin. He was one of the 'nice guys ' of life. He was a bachelor with a wide circle of friends. He was also one of the founders of the new little church from which the youth group came. He was popular with all, both young and old. His nephew was one of the passengers.

On the way home a drunken driver made a U-turn on a major motorway, drove up on the wrong side of the road and hit Clive's van head-on. My cousin was killed outright. Three of the children were killed. Clive's nephew was seriously injured and another young boy is confined to a wheelchair for life.

All this is terrible enough and not an uncommon experience in our world today. But the salt in the wound is that when the case was brought to court almost a year later, the drunken driver was given a minimal fine and a suspended sentence. This, in spite of a history of offences committed while driving under the influence of alcohol.

How do we deal with this? Do we deliberately nurture an ongoing bitterness because of the wrongness of the action and the lightness of the sentence? After all, who told him to get drunk? It was his choice. Not only that, but he had repeatedly broken the law and was no stranger to the courts. Every ounce of our beings wanted to protest against the sentence. In fact, we reasoned, wasn't he technically guilty of murder? Is not 'mitigating circumstances' a technicality devised by liberal lawmakers to remove the responsibility from the shoulders of the offender and blame it on society? It was an emotional struggle for all of us.

Something similar occurred after the massacre at our church. The sense of outrage from the nation was immense. We were visited by the State President and contacted by Dr Nelson Mandela and Dr Mangasuthu Buthelezi. We received messages from the Archbishop of Canterbury and the Pope. The Archbishop of Cape Town came to pray with me. Moslem and Jewish leaders came to our church to commiserate. They all expressed their anger not only at the violence but also at the sacrilege of an attack on the church. But inevitably the furore died down and the congregation was left to struggle with its grief and feelings of outrage. How were we to deal with this event from a spiritual as well as an emotional perspective?

The immediate response of the majority of the congregation was to offer forgiveness to the perpetrators. One of the most poignant images during that gut-wrenching time was to see Dawie Ackermann and his three children appear on TV. They were interviewed on the night of the attack. His wife Marita had been hit. Even before the paramedics appeared, Dawie realised she was dying. He managed to get her into a car and rushed her to the emergency unit of the hospital but they were too late. She was dead shortly after arrival.

Dawie returned to the church and was immediately surrounded by the media. With great calmness and peace in the midst of his personal storm, he and his children, Braam (20), Liezl (18) and Pierre (14), announced a refusal to seek revenge and offered forgiveness to the attackers. In a most moving way Dawie spoke of the forgiveness that was possible in Christ and invited the murderers of his beloved wife to turn to Christ. Nor was he alone in doing so.

Clive O'Kill and his wife Mary had recently left for England leaving 17-year-old Richard behind to finish his final year at high school. Richard died as he sheltered two young girls from the attackers' bullets. Clive too spoke of forgiveness. The tribute he paid to his son at the funeral was widely reported in the press and provided a most moving experience for thousands of people.

The same attitude was demonstrated by all interviewed at the time. One of the injured men was Gordon Bowers. He and his wife were both wounded. TV crews visited them at home a month after the event while they were still convalescing. Gordon was asked the question 'What would you do if you met your attackers face to face?' Who can forget that long, long moment before he replied; a moment made more agonising because of the intimate nature of TV. After what seemed like a great inner debate he replied, 'I would say, I am praying for you.'

A very cursory research into church history will reveal that the story of forgiveness being extended to those who persecute or injure is repeated many times. You may have experienced the ability to extend forgiveness in your own circumstances, but it is not an easy thing to do. Christians do not escape the struggle that goes with forgiveness when our suffering has been brought about by someone else.

In fact the offer of forgiveness by the victims of the massacre caused its own little storm. The media could not understand it. They kept coming back to this question of forgiveness. They wanted to know from me if I agreed with what the injured and bereaved were saying and if so, how I explained this attitude. I have referred to one BBC correspondent who asked me in a most perplexed manner, on a live link-up programme: 'Why are they forgiving these people? Surely they must feel anger? Why do they say these things?'

It is perfectly understandable for the non-Christian establishment to be confounded. Our news reports about trouble spots around the world are usually full of 'revenge attacks' and 'retaliation'. This is true of Ireland, Bosnia, the Middle East as well as South Africa. The response of these Christians stood in sharp contrast to that of many South African political figures and, on occasions, even some church leaders at the mass funerals of victims of violence in this country.

But quite apart from the media, many ordinary citizens were so outraged by this atrocity against our church that they were angry at us for offering forgiveness. The enormity of this crime in the context of South Africa and its politics quite overwhelmed them. They felt betrayed when we spoke words of forgiveness and restraint and appealed for reconciliation rather than revenge. Various letters were written to the press. One or two anonymous letters came my way, castigating us for our attitude. We received several abusive phone calls from strangers. One letter to a popular magazine captured the confusion and feelings of many others:

> How disgusted I am by Mr Dawie Ackermann's lack of feeling for his wife who died in the St James's Church massacre.
> How can he smile on TV and talk about her death in such a relaxed manner?
> If his wife had been maimed, like Dimitri Makagon, would he accept that in good faith too? He forgave the murderers, telling them so on television—who does he think he is, God?
> Being a Christian myself I just forgive members of my family who are nonbelievers and we'll all go to heaven one day. If a similar tragedy happened to one of them I would leave it to God to forgive, I most certainly would not.

Despite the confused nature of the comments in the letter, it nevertheless illustrates that forgiveness is a very emotional issue, one that is not clearly understood by all Christians. Yet the matter has to be faced.

A strange relationship

There is no ultimate victory over the consequences of tragedy and suffering until we have resolved the relationship issue. What does this mean? A crime of any nature or a deliberate injury inflicted on anyone establishes a personal relationship between the perpetrator and the victim.

This theme has been most ably expounded in David van Ness's excellent book entitled *Crime and its Victims*. He explains how modern criminal justice systems work. He shows how the crime is viewed by the courts as an offence against the *state* and not against the victim. The element of personal hurt and injury is virtually ignored. The courts do not seem to realise that a bizarre relationship has been established between the offender and his victim. The dimension of such a relationship is treated as nonexistent.

Because this is such an important concept and because he puts it so well in his book, I will let him speak for himself.

> It did not occur to us, or to the prosecutor or judge, that the criminal justice process we were a part of was divorced from the crimes which we and countless other victims had experienced. Technically, the defendants were not accused of robbing and beating other people. They were accused of breaking laws established by the state. The criminal justice system would not deal with the very real problem of the terrifying 'relationship' that had been created between those victims and the offenders during the burglary and assault.
>
> (Crime and its Victims, pp. 24–25)

Van Ness's argument is that the state deals simply with the act of crime but does not take into account the fact that a human dynamic has been released between the victim and the criminal. This dynamic can result in lifelong fear for the victim if the criminal is released or a lifelong search for revenge on behalf of the victim. Either way, these emotions can destroy our lives. Van Ness describes the cumulative effect of unresolved relationships in connection with crime as follows:

For one brief moment the victim and the offender confront each other. The crime establishes a relationship in which one wounds another. But we never deal with the wound. We try offenders when we catch them. And we sometimes send them to prison, not for the injury done to the victims, but because they broke the law. So now we have two wounds, and no healing.

The wounds multiply. Friends and neighbours of the victim, concerned for their own safety, start taking greater precautions. Fear is also a wound. The families of prisoners, unable to deal with the separation and stigma, begin to draw apart. Another wound. The victims who are reorganizing and the prisoners who are being released discover that the community cannot accept them as victims or ex-prisoners, and they conceal that part of themselves. More wounds.

We must hold offenders accountable. They have broken the law; they have hurt others.

If we do not insist that those who commit crimes be held responsible for their actions, we begin a slide into anarchy. But the offender can be held responsible in many ways. It is in our best interest to find those ways that heal wounds, not create new ones. (Ibid, pp. 54–55)

The point I am making is that human emotions are complex and are capable of hindering our progress in every area of life unless we deal with them properly. And the only proper way is to bring our feelings, reactions and emotions under the Lordship of Christ . This is also nec-

essary in the case of tragedy and suffering that is brought
about by someone else.

The governing principle

An important observation needs to be made. Most of
us act according to what we are by nature. In other words,
the great governing forces in our lives determine how we
respond to the crises we encounter. This means that for
some people life will always be evaluated in terms of money
and material things. For others life will be reckoned in
terms of status, prestige and position. Jesus put it another
way in Mark 7:21:

> For from within, out of men's hearts, come
> evil thoughts, sexual immorality, theft, mur-
> der, adultery . . .

Whatever is in your heart comes out in the unguarded
moments of life and especially in times of trial and trouble.
The governing principle in your life will be the means by
which you measure the suffering that you experience. In
our hour of need our people spoke from an inner spiritual
perspective. They had come to understand the real issues of
life. They had been taught that the greatest value in life is to
obey God and to live for him. The gospel with its great
eternal realities was rooted in them. Thus when they were
interviewed they spoke quite spontaneously from that perspective. In other words, they were simply being who they
are—Christians. There was nothing artificial about their attitudes, pain and grief, nor about their offer of forgiveness.

Instinctively they seemed to realise that a relationship
had been established between them and the attackers. They
knew that there was a possibility that sooner or later they

might need to face these men in a court of law. This new 'relationship' had to be dealt with; it was a battle they had to fight. They chose the option of forgiveness. It was artless and without any coaching or prompting. It was the simple outworking of the gospel in their lives.

There are many people who have the same experience. They simply refuse to let the root of bitterness take hold. If they do, that root will become a plant that will grow and finally choke anything else in their lives.

This illustrates another area of difference between Christians and non-Christians. It highlights the transformation that occurs in the life of the man or woman who has experienced the new birth and surrendered to the Lordship of Christ. Christ rules in our hearts and lives. He did not retaliate when He was reviled and crucified and He taught His followers to do the same.

This instinct was displayed on the night of the attack. Some people queried this response by suggesting that it was in fact a reaction from shock. They suggested that the peculiar circumstances and the consequent flow of adrenaline was largely responsible for this attitude. We readily agreed that to a large extent the responses were indeed made during the shock of the ordeal. But this did not lessen the sincerity or the reality of the attitude of Christian meekness, self-control and non-retaliation. We fully expected that those who displayed such attitudes would need to cope with the normal effects of grief sooner or later as the shock wore off. This in fact happened. Even now at the time of writing some of the bereaved are coping with a very deep level of grief and loss. But even so there has been no change in their basic attitude of forgiveness. They remain true to their instincts and act according to the new spiritual nature within them because they are Christians.

Not least among these new instincts is the realisation that they and the attackers have a 'relationship' that needs to be faced. This came to the fore when some weeks later arrests were made and an identification parade was arranged. About forty of the victims were asked to attend and almost without exception they experienced a heightened sense of nervousness and dread. For the first time they came face to face with men who could possibly be the killers.

The dynamics of 'relationship' with the perpetrators was further illustrated in the way the congregation began to pray for the killers. This was done in our Sunday congregations as well as in our various prayer meetings. We asked God to bring the criminals not only to justice but to repentance.

We felt a special responsibility to pray for them. It seemed to us as if the whole country was hating them. Somebody needed to pray for them; so we did. This is not mentioned to indicate how specially holy the congregation is but rather to illustrate the truth of the observation made by Van Ness about a relationship being established between the criminal and his victim. That relationship exists and needs to be resolved. You may find this to be true in your own personal tragedy or suffering. If you have been raped, mugged, burgled, beaten by your husband or cheated by a friend, there is a relationship to be sorted out. It is one thing for the state to bring the offender to book and to sentence him to a period of imprisonment, but there is still the sense that there is something unresolved between you and the offender. Although Van Ness writes largely about the American criminal system, his basic thesis is universally true.

How do we as Christians resolve this strange relationship problem? How do we handle it? The answer is that sooner or later we must face the challenge of forgiveness. Forgiveness has far more to it than meets the eye. From a Christian point of view it needs to be clearly understood so that we can avoid the trap of oversimplicity or sentimentalism. To the outsider it may appear almost as if we are simply overlooking or condoning the crime. At the same time we cannot avoid the clear teaching of Scripture that forgiveness is one of the chief ways in which we display to others our own relationship to God.

Aspects of forgiveness

One of the difficulties in thinking through the issue of Christian forgiveness is the fact that there are at least three different levels of offences and each of these levels demands a different facet of forgiveness. Some offences are committed against God and therefore require God's forgiveness. Other offences are civil or social and therefore require a different treatment. A third category is personal forgiveness which is required when crimes are committed against me personally.

Let me assert right away that all wrong actions are offences against God. That is why we need the atoning death of Christ on the cross. We cannot experience God's forgiveness until our sins have been dealt with. But while that is true at the spiritual level, there is also the area of offences which need either the punishment of the state or some form of restitution to be made to the victim. It will help us to understand the complexities of the issue if we bear these different aspects in mind.

Atonement means a covering or protection. This is what Christ did for us on the cross. He covers us with His righteousness so that we are delivered from the judgement of God. Forgiveness means that charges are dropped because the demands of the law have been satisfied or restitution has been offered. Forgiveness in the accurate sense always requires repentance and restitution because it is always an offence against God as well as against a human being.

Why do we do wrong things in the first place? It is because we have a bias deep within us that seeks self-satisfaction. The Bible calls this bias sin. Sin is a principle lodged in our very natures. There is nothing that God can do with this but judge it, which is exactly what He did in Christ on the cross. And it is precisely because our sins have been judged, atonement has been made and satisfaction offered that forgiveness can be extended. But what happens when criminals commit the kind of deed perpetrated at St James? If they had to repent before God, does that mean that they should not be held accountable? If a rapist says in court that he has come to his senses and sees how wrong he is and that he has now become a Christian, should he be let off the hook?

At least part of the answer can be seen in the way the Old Testament dealt with offenders. The relationship between the offender and the offended was recognised. Although it was possible for an offender to be reinstated religiously, he still had a responsibility to the victim. He had to make some form of restitution. A quick look through Exodus 22 as an example will confirm this. The dynamic between the two parties had to be recognised and dealt with.

In the same way crime has to be dealt with at different levels. It has to be dealt with theologically, in relation to God. It has to be dealt with socially or civilly, in relation to the community, and it has to be dealt with personally, in relation to the victim.

In what way then can it be said that the members of St James 'forgave' their attackers? Was the crime not more than an attack against the church? Firstly, the members of the church could obviously not offer any 'theological' forgiveness. In other words, they could not speak for God. The crimes committed that night were not committed against the congregation alone but against God. His laws were broken. The forgiveness offered was therefore not a spiritual forgiveness in the sense that their sins were atoned for and blotted out. Only God can do that. We see that both Christ and Stephen prayed for 'God' to forgive their murderers (Luke 23:34; Acts 7: 60).

Secondly, let us look at the personal relationship of the victim to the perpetrator. Forgiveness is dependent on repentance. The act of forgiveness is extended to brothers and even then the notion of repentance and restitution is implied.

In Matthew 18:21–35 we have a famous passage on our Lord's teaching about forgiveness. It contains the well-known parable about the king and his servant who owed him a debt he could not repay. The king's patience with the man is based on his request: 'Be patient with me and I will pay back everything' (verse 26). In other words there was an acknowledgement of debt and responsibility. There was a plea for mercy (verse 32). The servant was ultimately condemned because he showed no real change of heart as was illustrated by his dealings with a fellow servant who owed him a lesser sum. Our Lord was dealing with our attitudes to each other as 'fellow servants' or brothers (verse 35). We should act towards each other as God has acted towards us.

What then about unbelievers who harm us, those who are not our brothers? Except for the reference in the Lord's Prayer in Matthew 6: 12–14 where the word 'forgiveness' is used, most references to forgiveness are made in the context of the Christian family. However, we must not press this too far because the attitude of forgiveness, even to unbelievers, is distinctly Christian.

It is important to remember that, in the strict sense of the word, only God can truly forgive. It is also important to bear in mind that forgiveness needs to be received and that to receive it implies repentance and reconciliation.

This obviously does not always happen between Christians and those who do them harm. Thus the Bible casts the attitude of forgiveness to unbelievers in a positive way. In other words, we cannot force anyone to say, 'I'm sorry.' Nor can we force anyone to be reconciled to us. So in a strict sense 'forgiveness' is not possible. However the Christian maintains the attitude of forgiveness and conciliation towards the unbeliever who has harmed him.

The Scriptures instruct Christians to love and not hate their enemies, and to pray for those who abuse them (Matthew 5:43–44; Luke 6:27–28). But pray for what? Pray for their repentance and true turning to God.

Having said that, let's ask why it is that Christians are to be non-retaliatory. The reason is that we lose our credibility as the alternative society if we behave exactly as other people do. Part of our witness to Christ and his saving grace is an attitude of meekness. In other words the entire mission of the church, the witness of the gospel, is affected if Christians give in to retaliation or revenge. This is illustrated by the example of our Lord Jesus in 1 Peter 2:21–24 and 1 Peter 4:1–7.

How do Christians respond to evil? We respond personally and in our personal capacity we refuse the path of revenge. We do not return evil for evil. Rather, we bless those who curse us and pray for those who persecute us (1 Peter 3:9; Matthew 5:44). As individuals we remember that we are disciples of Christ and our response must reflect that. We are to remember the injunction of James 1:19–20:

> My dear brothers, take note of this: Everyone should be quick to listen, slow to speak and slow to become angry, for man's anger does not bring about the righteous life that God desires.

After the attack on our church there were many who would have wanted to act in anger against the perpetrators. Scripture refuses to sanction this because it has a negative impact on our mission. Our wrath does not bring about the righteousness that we desire in society. Acting in wrath and anger only continues the cycle of violence. As individuals then we have a different spirit.

But thirdly, we do not act only in a personal capacity. We are also citizens who must desire and pray for the civil authorities to reward the good and punish the evildoer for the sake of others (Romans 13:1–7). The wider community dimension must be taken into consideration These criminals broke the laws of society.

In other words, a Christian has no real power to forgive anybody in the judicial sense of the word. Just as the congregation had no power to forgive them on God's behalf, so they also had no power to offer 'civil' forgiveness. The crime committed that night was a crime against the entire community. The laws of society were broken as well as the laws of God. There is a civil dimension, a judicial element that has entered into the picture. The state must take action against the perpetrators. The sufferers have no power to offer forgiveness on the part of the state.

That was not what was meant when the members of the church so spontaneously said they forgave the attackers. But they did offer forgiveness in their personal capacity as individual Christians. They were following the injunctions of Jesus who said:

> For if you forgive men when they sin against you, your heavenly Father will also forgive you.
>
> (Matthew 6:14)

The same teaching is repeated several times in the gospels (Matthew 18:21–22; Mark 11:25; Luke 17:3).

If forgiveness presupposes repentance and restitution, the forgiveness Christians offer is not an absolving of sins before God. In our case there was no religious sentiment which prevented us from laying a charge against the perpetrators before the Almighty, implying that even he should let the crime pass. Nor was there a suggestion that the law should not take its course. Sometimes people thought this was what we meant. They thought we were condoning the act by offering 'forgiveness'. There was such a sense of community outrage that people felt we were speaking on behalf of the community by stating that we forgave the criminals. But this is far from the truth which we went to great lengths to explain to the media.

Rather, the congregation meant to convey their refusal to take private revenge or to fall into the destructive snare of becoming bitter. We refused to join in the outcry for revenge. There was an honest and spontaneous attempt to use the disaster to display the true spirit of Christ. We remembered that we ourselves were offenders against God and that we had been forgiven freely by His grace. Our forgiveness of our attackers was not to exonerate them from their sin or responsibility but to demonstrate to them the different nature displayed by those who have themselves been forgiven by God. Our attitude was meant to be an invitation to them to come before God in true penitence and to seek His forgiveness. It was a conscious though spontaneous attempt to reflect the words of the apostle Peter in 1 Peter 2:21—23:

> To this you were called, because Christ suffered for you, leaving you an example, that you should follow in His steps.
> He committed no sin,
> and no deceit was found in His mouth.'
> When they hurled their insults at Him, He

did not retaliate; when He suffered, he made
no threats. Instead, he entrusted Himself to
Him who judges justly.

How else could we deal with the relationship that had
been brought into existence between us and the criminals? We could have chosen to live with hatred and bitterness. To deny that there was some sort of relationship
would only have increased our emotional difficulties. Instead we recognised that a dynamic had been brought
into existence. We chose to deal with it by means of forgiveness. Not, I repeat, by condoning their actions but
rather by a conscious and deliberate decision not to harbour revenge. Instead we prayed for two things. Firstly,
that they would be brought to repentance and secondly,
that they would be brought to justice.

We do not believe they should escape the consequences
of their crime. We honestly believe they should face the
full force of the law. Yet we feel an obligation to love our
enemies as our Master taught us, and to pray for them.
Even if they were caught and punished, we would want
the opportunity to face them, pray for them and minister
to them if that were possible.

However, the question remains: How is it possible to
maintain this kind of spiritual and emotional equilibrium?
The answer lies in the firm conviction that there will be a
day of judgement.

Judgement

The coming day of judgement is a doctrine that has
been abused, misunderstood and often used to manipu-
late people. But correctly understood in the context of
God's character and justice, it is a doctrine full of comfort

for Christians. On that day justice will at last be seen to be done. All the longings of our hearts for God to 'do something' will find fulfilment then. It is the explanation we all need to explain the seemingly long delays by God in acting on behalf of His beleaguered children.

No one ultimately gets away with any wrongdoing. All those millions of people through the centuries who seemed to have everything their own way, who have often been guilty of the most monstrous crimes against humanity, finally get to face God.

The day of judgement is not a delayed day of revenge for Christians. We must be careful that we do not adopt the attitude that says, 'We won't get them, but you get them God!' That is wrong and it is a way of covering up a spirit of revenge. Although we must leave vengeance to God, who alone has the right to take it, the Christian may still cry for justice. Revelation 6:10 says:

> They called out in a loud voice, 'How long, Sovereign Lord, holy and true, until you judge the inhabitants of the earth and avenge our blood?'

We must keep the distinction clear between the desire for vengeance and the longing for justice. Christians do not surrender the right to justice or the search for justice in any given situation. But the Christian's desire for justice is not based on a secret vindictive desire to see the offender get what he deserves. Rather it is because we realise that the offender has broken the law of God. We realise that society cannot continue with any form or order if offenders are not caught and punished.

The day of judgement is simply a day of reckoning, of justice, of the display of the righteous character of God as he calls sinners to account. That is why Christians do not need to fret. We often feel fretful in the face of injustice because our instinctive desire to see wrong punished seems to be doomed to frustration. But we know that the day is coming. We can afford to wait. We will not give in to the lower nature of retaliation and revenge. Rather, we follow the example of Jesus and exercise self-restraint. We will not contribute to the culture of violence and hatred sweeping our world but rather we will attempt to be peacemakers.

This characteristic of Christians is what Jesus described as 'meekness' in Matthew 5:5. There is a vast difference between meekness and weakness. Meekness is the self-imposed restraint exercised by Christians so that Christ may be glorified in their lives.

We recognise that the people who have hurt us now have a relationship with us. Sometimes this relationship is one of fear and horror . We deal with this relationship by refusing to be intimidated or to retaliate. We extend forgiveness to them in the sense of non-retaliation and a refusal to entertain bitterness. We pray for them and seek the salvation of their souls. Still we require that the state should bring them to book for their crimes and that, for the sake of order in society, they should pay for their crimes. And in the event of the perpetrators of evil escaping justice in this life, we rest secure in the knowledge that justice will yet be seen to be done when they finally have to answer to God Almighty, the Judge of all the earth.

Steps to forgiveness

Having concentrated on the responses that were drawn from people in our own situation, let me now turn to you, the reader, and the personal tragedy you may be dealing with in your own life or in the life of a loved one.

Sometimes the experiences of others can appear to be so remote from our own situation. We read marvellous stories of how others coped and instead of helping us, they make us feel more wretched and miserable than before. I want to encourage you not to measure yourself against anyone else. Remember that your temperament and reactions will be different from those of other people. Your duty is not to imitate someone else but to try, in spite of your pain, to imitate Christ. It is true that others who have been through great trials can be an inspiration to us. But we must be careful to keep the distinction between being inspired and encouraged by others and the subtle danger of trying to emulate them.

When it comes to the matter of forgiveness, we often struggle to reconcile our desire to demonstrate true Christianity with our emotions of anger and fear. It may be helpful to summarise the steps we need to take to offer forgiveness to those who harm us.

First, we must understand that 'a new undesirable relationship comes into being between an offender and a victim'. Let me point out that this occurs even in something as common as the unfaithfulness of a spouse. If one of the partners is unfaithful, it brings a new dynamic into the relationship. It is in fact a new relationship within a relationship. Something has happened that affects the way the two people relate to each other. It is true even if the marriage was filled with conflict and unhappiness. Sexual unfaithfulness on the part of one or both of the spouses brings an additional complication into the situation. The same holds true for any kind of crime or pain inflicted by one human being on another, be it rape, incest, fraud and cheating or the sort of attack perpetrated by terrorists and violent criminals.

By the word 'relationship' I am not referring to the kind of relationship that exists between friends, lovers or colleagues. This would be a horrific idea to any victim. Rather I am referring to the fact that something personal has taken place between two people that needs to be resolved. And unless this personal element is recognised, the issue simply will not be overcome.

The question then becomes 'How am I going to deal with this personal element that has come unbidden into my life?' We can choose to seek revenge and retaliation. We can choose to brood, sink into self-pity and become unbearable. We can also choose to be fearful and neurotic for the rest of our days. But the better way is to choose to face the problem and decide to exercise the option of forgiveness thereby resolving our reaction to our enemy. The idea of a relationship, then, is a key concept in the struggle to forgive.

Secondly, you need to remember that *by choosing to forgive you are not condoning what happened*. This is a mistake many people make. Christian forgiveness does not say `What you did is okay'. On the contrary, it says `What you did is not okay. It was wrong and wicked and deserves to be punished. But I myself won't punish you. I will leave it to the law and to God.'

In other words, when Christians offer forgiveness they are simply saying 'I do not seek personal revenge, but I do seek justice'. Forgiveness does not imply that the normal course of the law should not be carried out. Rather it seeks for the punishment of the offender in an orderly way so that society is not disrupted any further. Thus Christians seek for justice but not revenge.

In the third place, we remember that *for true forgiveness to be received there has to be repentance and, as far as possible, restitution*. Forgiveness is free but not unconditional. The fact is, however, that often the culprits get away with their crimes. It is not always possible to obtain repentance from offenders or to get adequate restitution.

What are Christians then to do? We have no control over the responses of others. We cannot force people to repent or to make restitution. Therefore we can only display the Christian virtue of non-retaliation and self-control. We seek to follow the example of Christ who, when He was reviled, did not retaliate. In this way we reflect our own relationship to God who forgives us our trespasses on the basis of Christ's atonement and our repentance brought about by the sovereign work of the Holy Spirit in our hearts.

By way of example consider a case of divorce that is full of acrimony. Assuming that one spouse is innocent and the other guilty of the marriage breakdown, the innocent Christian spouse can only make offer of forgiveness. This forgiveness can only be received if the guilty spouse repents. If that does not happen, it goes to court. The innocent spouse then seeks justice in the form of an equitable agreement. The innocent party does not say 'I forgive you. Have your own way. Everything is okay.' Rather the message to the guilty spouse is 'What you did is wrong. I will forgive you if you repent and put the wrong things right. But if you don't, I will attempt to get justice through the courts.'

The same principle applies in all of life. The Christian is always willing to extend forgiveness. It is however not always received. But for Christians the actions of retaliation and revenge are not options. Rather we seek to reflect our commitment to Christ in all our reactions, because we know that our ability to deal with others in this way is a sign that we ourselves have been forgiven.

Some readers may find this a very difficult exercise. When you reflect on the hurt and heartache that has been caused you, not to mention the financial cost and emotional trauma, it is not easy to think in such cool terms about forgiveness and reactions because we are reacting with our hearts. We need to bear in mind that the choice to respond as a Christian is primarily a choice of the mind, not of the emotions. We need to remember that God deals with us primarily through our thinking processes. There is always a battle going on between the mind and the heart and I am only too aware of the fact that the heart often wins. We often make wrong choices be cause we evaluate things emotionally rather than intellectually. But when it comes to dealing with those who have inflicted pain upon us, we simply must keep our emotions in check. It may take a while before we can get our emotions under control. That is why it is important not to make any major decisions immediately after we have suffered trauma. Allow some time to pass.

The decision to forgive someone is made in the area of our thinking and our wills, not in the area of our feelings. Left to our feelings, we would never forgive others. This may in fact account for at least some of the tension Christians feel about the matter of forgiveness. They have wrongly assumed that forgiveness includes a new set of feelings that is free of hurt and anger when, in fact, they feel exactly the opposite. In this way their struggles are intensified because they are trying to do something that is not only impossible but is also not demanded by the Scriptures. It must be something we 'will' to do because we are Christians. It is a decision to deal with an abnormal relationship by exercising the Christian option of non-retaliation and the offer of forgiveness to the offender.

But what happens if the perpetrator gets away with what he has done? What about all those husbands and wives who have broken up their homes and left devastated families behind while they seem to enjoy a new and exciting life? What about the millions of tyrants, murderers and despots who have the blood of millions on their hands? This forms the next step in forgiveness. We remind ourselves that we can afford the option of non-retaliation because *God has a day when He himself, through Christ, will judge the world*. We must believe this. It is the only way to make sense of our unjust and perverse world. If there were no such event pending, nothing would matter any more. But such a day is coming. We must simply wait.

In the meantime, although we may be struggling with our emotions, we will continue to treat even our enemies with human dignity. We will not sink to their level by retaliating. We will treat them without hatred or bitterness. We remember that God harbours no bitterness against us even though we were once enemies and rebels. We remember that He is good to the just and the unjust, that even wicked people enjoy His general blessings upon the world. But we recall that they will one day answer to Him. On that day, all the accounts will be settled.

8

What About the Devil?

While this book was being written, a sensational murder trial was unfolding in Cape Town. Two teenage lovers killed the girl's mother in a most brutal way and tried to bury her body in a shallow grave in their backyard. What made the trial especially significant was the fact that they were blaming the devil as an official defence strategy.

I know that people have often claimed to be under the power of an evil force when committing a crime. In fact a South African Prime Minister was stabbed to death years ago by a man claiming that inner voices told him to do it. But this was the first time in the legal history of our country that demon possession was pleaded as a mitigating factor. It was taken seriously in court arguments. This fact seems to indicate that in many parts of the world there is a gradual departure from the prevailing secular view which held any belief in the supernatural to be totally invalid.

Many Christian thinkers are re-examining the implications of a Western world-view which largely affects our understanding of both human beings and the world they live in. This view usually excludes the spiritual dimension of our being. Either we go to the one extreme of saying that there are no supernatural forces in the world or we go to the other extreme of seeing a demon in every unpleasant event in life. We are now hearing calls for a more balanced view.

Man is not merely a physical being. He is also a spiritual

being—that means he has a spirit as well as a body. Similarly, his world consists of more than that which can be seen. There are dimensions to God's creation which are supernatural and cannot be detected through the normal channels.

All this raises many intriguing questions about our Christian faith and the struggles we have in this world. Many books have been written on spiritual warfare and several books have explored the mysterious subject of the devil and demonology. What role does he play in this world and, more particularly, what role does he play in the suffering and trials of God's people?

The conquest of the devil

We start our enquiry by examining the Christian claim that the devil has been conquered. The New Testament claims that on the cross, Christ triumphed over the devil. This is the way the apostle Paul states it in Colossians 2:13–15:

> When you were dead in your sins and in the uncircumcision of your sinful nature, God made you alive with Christ. He forgave us all our sins, having cancelled the written code, with its regulations, that was against us and that stood opposed to us; He took it away, nailing it to the cross. And having disarmed the powers and authorities, He made a public spectacle of them, triumphing over them by the cross.

While for many years it has been considered sophisticated and intellectually respectable to ridicule belief in a personal devil and the existence of demons, the new mood of religious pluralism and acceptance of the validity of the beliefs of other religions has undermined this view. As the East and its religious practices has invaded the West, and the rise of acceptance of African traditional religion with its emphasis on ancestral spirits has become more prominent, so a new, if wary, credulity has arisen. This makes it all the more important for Christians to understand in what sense it can be said that the devil is conquered. For if it is true, as Christians affirm, that he is indeed defeated, how do we explain his presence and ongoing activity in the world today?

I want to refer to the well-known British preacher, theologian and author, Dr John Stott, to assist us at this point. In his classic book *The Cross of Christ*, Dr Stott makes the clear statement that the decisive defeat of Satan took place at the cross. His very helpful explanation shows how the conquest of Satan is depicted in Scripture as unfolding in six stages (pp. 227ff). Let us look at these stages to gain an overall perspective of the devil's defeat. Firstly, Stott points out that the conquest over Satan was *predicted*. The first prediction took place in the Garden of Eden and was given by God Himself:

> And I will put enmity
> between you and the woman,
> and between your offspring and hers;
> he will crush your head,
> and you will strike his heel.
> (Genesis 3:15)

The woman's seed has been identified as the Messiah by whom Satan is finally crushed and the rule of evil eradicated. All other references to the rule of God in the Old Testament may be understood as prophecies of the ultimate defeat of Satan.

The second stage was *the beginning of the conquest brought about by the ministry of Jesus*. Satan made many attempts to get rid of Jesus or to deflect Him from His task. Herod's murder of the children in Bethlehem; the temptations in the wilderness; the further temptations by the crowd to force Jesus into fulfilling the popular notion of a political messiah; Peter's apparent denial of the necessity of the cross and, finally, the actual challenge to come down from the cross to convince the crowd are among the many features of Satan's struggle against his own ultimate overthrow by Jesus.

The third stage was *the actual defeat of Satan on the cross*. Jesus said that the 'prince of this world' would be condemned (John 12:31; 14:30; 16:11). He finally destroyed Satan by His atoning and substitutionary death (Hebrews 2:14–15).

Coming back to the apostle Paul's words in Colossians 2:13–15, we note two aspects of Christ's saving work on the cross: the forgiveness of sins and the cosmic overthrow of the principalities and powers—supernatural spiritual agencies such as Satan and demons. Others may have a different interpretation for the phrase 'principalities and powers', but the argument in favour of regarding them as satanic agents is very convincing.

The victory over Satan predicted by God immediately after the fall was decisively won on the cross.

But fourthly, the victory over Satan was *confirmed and declared at the resurrection*. We must be careful to bear in mind that it was on the cross that the victory was won, not at the resurrection. The resurrection endorsed and proclaimed the victory of the cross. It is impossible to think or preach accurately about the cross without the resurrection, for both events together constitute the basis of our salvation. However we must emphasise that evil agents were deprived of their powers at the cross. It was there that they were crushed. The resurrection was the glorious demonstration of Calvary's victory.

In the fifth stage, the conquest of Satan is seen as *an ongoing event as Christians begin to witness in the power of the Spirit and preach Christ to people.* Every single person who turns to Christ constitutes another piece of evidence of the great victory won at Calvary. The devil's power is confronted by the power of the gospel in that person's life and the individual is enabled to turn from darkness to light, from Satan to God. Thus Satan, who is already defeated, is further defeated as the kingdom of God advances in the world.

The final stage of Satan's doom occurs at *the second coming of Christ*, the *parousia*. On that day every knee will bow to Him and every tongue will confess Him as Lord. The devil will be thrown into the lake of fire. All evil dominion and power will be finally destroyed. The Son will hand over the kingdom to the Father so that God may be 'all in all' (1 Corinthians 15:24–28).

The problem for us living in this world of suffering is the interim period between stages five and six. Most Christians have no difficulty in understanding the biblical prophecies of Satan's ultimate doom. But many believers are confused by the apparent contradiction between the statements of Satan's great defeat at the cross and the evidence of the seemingly formidable power he still wields today. We know and believe that he will be finally overthrown at the second coming of our Lord and Saviour, but how do we explain his power between these two events?

Our 'interim' struggle

The important principle for us to grasp is that, although the devil has been defeated, he has not yet surrendered or conceded defeat. Nor will he. We know from the Bible that he will fight to the bitter end when he is finally cast into the abyss. Although he has in fact been overthrown, he is not yet eliminated from the scene and he continues to wield great power. Thus we struggle with a tension in our Christian life. We know, on the one hand that, having been converted, we belong to God's flock and will be kept safe. Yet on the other hand we are warned by Paul about the principalities and powers with which we wrestle (Ephesians 6:10–17). Peter exhorts us to resist the devil who is like a roaring lion, walking around seeking whom he may devour (1 Peter 5:8). These are fearsome pictures which we must understand.

Some Christians respond to this tension by becoming 'demon conscious' and ascribing all the woes of life to the devil. They see the devil behind everything and they sometimes teeter on the brink of paranoia. They believe fervently in Christ's victory over the devil but engage in actions to counter the devil which border on the ludicrous. They see themselves as having the same authority as Jesus had and which He passed on to the apostles. They therefore engage in exorcisms which consist sometimes of prayer and fasting. Often these exorcisms are accompanied by verbal attacks and rebukes of the devil with demands for him to let go and depart from either the afflicted person or the troublesome situation.

I do not decry any attempt at loosening the hold of the Evil One in any situation. On the contrary I support all attempts to prayerfully seek the deliverance of those afflicted by the devil. However this approach does raise some important questions. The first of these is *the kind of authority the followers of Jesus possess*. Often an appeal is made to Matthew 28:18–20 to support the idea that all disciples of Christ have the same kind of authority that Jesus had and which His disciples displayed. There are however two important points to make concerning this passage of Scripture. The first is that the authority has been given to Jesus, not to us. He is the one who wields great power and supremacy in the universe. The second point is that because He has authority, He commissions us to go and make disciples. But how? By teaching. In other words, Christ confronts the powers of darkness to-day through the gospel. When He was on earth He confronted demon powers personally. Now He confronts them through His Word proclaimed and taught.

Sometimes Christians fail to recognise the extent of Christ's victory on the cross. They appear to limit it to the forgiveness of the sins of the believer. But we are told that Christ's work on the cross had very far-reaching implications, even for the powers of darkness. Paul refers to these powers having been 'disarmed':

> And having disarmed the powers and authorities, He made a public spectacle of them, triumphing over them by the cross. (Colossians 2:15)

Thus the proclamation of the cross and the great victory it represents is to confront the powers and principalities with the same Jesus who was encountered on earth, but now crucified and risen. It is in this sense that authority is passed on to His disciples.

But this will raise another questions. *What about the references to the disciples* in Matthew 10:1 and Mark 6:7 where they are specifically given authority over evil spirits? The problem with this is that it takes a unique event in the life of Christ and the training of His disciples and makes it the norm for the church. The Gospels intend to show us that Christ defeated the enemy decisively at the cross. The exorcisms are sacraments or symbols of this event.

They were not events to be copied by the followers of Christ any more than the raising of Eutychus from the dead by the apostle Paul (Acts 20:7–12). These were unique displays of God's power which validated the call and authority of the apostles. There are no successors to the apostles today who have the same unique authority. Our authority today lies in the gospel—the preached Word of God.

This is an important concept to grasp. The gospel itself is the great 'exorcist'. The gospel's power to deliver from the powers of darkness is clearly referred to by the apostle Paul in Acts 26:18. He describes the gospel he preached as 'opening their eyes and turning them from darkness to light, and from the power of Satan to God.' This is repeated by the great apostle in a different way in Colossians 1:13:

> For He has rescued us from the dominion of
> darkness and brought us into the kingdom
> of the Son He loves.

Here we are told clearly that Jesus has rescued us from the rule, the dominion of darkness. Its hold is broken by our redemption and forgiveness of sins.

A third question that needs to be addressed is *the narrow view of Satan's activities* entertained by some Christians. Some see his activities almost exclusively in terms of physical possession and emotional oppression. But his most dangerous activity by far is described by the apostle Paul in 1 Timothy 4:1:

> The Spirit clearly says that in the later times
> some will abandon the faith and follow de-
> ceiving spirits and things taught by demons.

Deliverance is therefore not only from possession but also from wrong doctrines. Evil spirits do not only possess, they also deceive. The antidote to this too is the public reading of Scripture, preaching and teaching (1 Timothy 4:13).

In the New Testament there is in fact little evidence apart from Christ Himself and the apostles, that the devil is to be rebuked and commanded to 'come out'. Apart from the well-known incident in Acts 16, there is of course the reference to the sons of Sceva in Acts 19. There are also two other passing references in the Gospels, one by Jesus in Matthew 12:27 which seems to refer to some form of exorcism that was practised by the Jews. The other reference to exorcism is made by the disciple John in Mark 9:38 where he refers to someone not of the group of disciples who was using Jesus' name to cast out evil spirits. There is another reference in Acts 5: 16 to miracles worked by Peter, including exorcisms. It is in the context of the general authority of his apostleship and signifies the supernatural authority that the gospel possesses and that Peter is Christ's authorised representative.

These interesting references highlight the fact that the activities many engage in today are not what was envisaged in the Scriptures. Rather the preaching of the gospel and the consistent teaching of God's Word carries the power and the authority of Jesus to drive out darkness.

This, however, raises another question. *What about demon possession today?* Is there such a thing and how do we deal with it? Quite obviously there is demon possession today and no doubt, as the influence of the gospel recedes, there seems to be an increase in the influence of the powers of darkness. Wherever the gospel is not known, the enemy holds sway. As the gospel is proclaimed, so the enemy reacts. This probably accounts for the numerous reports of demon possession related in the Gospels. The murder case referred to at the beginning of this chapter illustrates the rise in occultic interest and demonic activity. I do not want to suggest that there is no point in confronting these evil forces. Obviously we must do so. I simply want to plead for a biblical approach to this subject and not the unthinking approach adopted by some people who nevertheless mean well.

We are called to pray for all men. In fact, in that portion of Scripture called the Lord's Prayer, Jesus taught us to pray 'deliver us from the evil one' (Matthew 5:13). There is some debate about whether the phrase should read 'from evil' or 'from the evil one'. If the latter is correct, as I believe it is, it is an indication of how we are to approach the problem of Satan's attacks upon us. It is by fervent prayer, faith in Christ's power and authority and the clear teaching of God's Word.

We are not to adopt an attitude of defeatism and resignation which awaits the final overthrow of Satan and sees no hope of victory in this world. Such people often become uninvolved in any of the great struggles in which we as Christians are called to engage. They see no point in it. A form of passive piety develops which is equally wrong. We are after all not passive as Christians. We have a glorious message to proclaim. Nor are we without help. We have great spiritual resources in Christ to whom we can turn. Nor are we without hope, for He has promised never to leave us or forsake us. Rather, he Has promised to be with us in our ministries to win the world until the end of the age.

We need to understand that the tension between the victory of Christ over the devil and the experience we have in this world is what Bible scholars describe as the 'already' and the 'not yet'. In other words, the Bible teaches that the kingdom of God has *already* been introduced into this world and is steadily advancing as the years go by. We are *already* God's sons and daughters. We have *already* experienced His redeeming power and freedom from the slavery of sin and guilt. But the old age of darkness has *not yet* completely passed. God's kingdom has *not yet* arrived in all its fullness. There is in fact an overlap of the new period of God's rule and the old dispensation of darkness and rebellion. Thus we live in the interim period. During this time the devil is still very active although He was decisively defeated at Calvary.

This 'interim' struggle is illustrated in our personal salvation. During this interim period we receive the new birth but also discover that our fallen natures—our old sinful natures—continue to assert themselves so that we often have to struggle with ourselves. The same applies to Christ's victory over death. We know that death has been conquered for all who believe in Christ, yet we still have to die. In this way, the old enemies still exist. Their power has been broken but they have not yet been banished from the earth.

If we understand this, it will keep us from becoming triumphalistic. Triumphalism conveys the idea that Christians should always be victorious over both the devil and the circumstances of life. It assumes that the final victory which will be ours after Christ's return is in fact available now. In its extreme forms, this attitude results in the claim that Christians should never be in any sort of trouble. They should never be ill and they should never struggle financially as others do. Rather they should always be rejoicing, confident, happy and living above their circumstances. This is a stance that can result in arrogance, disillusionment when we discover from the experiences of life that this is just not true, and finally defeat.

It will also help us to understand how it is possible for the devil to be active in the world although he has been defeated. We struggle against an enemy who has been overthrown but not yet abolished from the earth. He is malevolent and deceitful and still seems able to wield great power to inflict harm on the human race and to deceive people into believing lies. While we live in this 'interim' period—the period before his final doom—we need to be alert and watchful.

The devil's schemes

The apostle Paul urges us to 'put on the full armour of God so that you can take your stand against the devil's schemes' (Ephesians 6:11). Our enemy is a crafty, intelligent and thinking creature who appears to have many ways of tempting the children of God . He confuses people and blinds them to the truth, disrupting the work of God and wooing people from the gospel.

It would be outside the scope of this book to work systematically through the Scriptures to compile a catalogue of the devil's activities. My main concern is to pose the question: 'What role does the devil play in tragedy?' Many people told me that the massacre on our church was an attack of the devil. While the broad statement is accepted, we need to be careful how we approach this subject.

People who have experienced tragedy in their lives may be further traumatised by well-meaning people who assure them that their trouble is inspired by Satan. They are told that he can be overcome by prayer and 'resisting the devil'. This often takes the form of verbal shouts at Satan to depart.

I have had to deal with people who had been deeply hurt by the pending break-up of a marriage. In their distress, they have been further hurt by people who have told them that the situation is of the devil and that by exercising faith, the problem could be reversed. Who wouldn't respond to that if their partner was on the verge of walking out? The problem is that no matter how much faith you exercise, the marriage still disintegrates. The hurting spouse now carries the added burden of guilt for not having enough faith.

The same applies to people with devastating illnesses. Often they have to endure long times of prayer and 're-buking the devil', only to see no change in the situation. Then they are told that the real problem lies with them. They do not have enough faith and are therefore responsible for their own illness. This is not only unbiblical, it is heartless and cruel.

On the other hand, what pastor has not encountered people who have put up with the most horrendous things in their lives without making an effort to correct them, under the mistaken impression it is the Lord's will. I have met Christians who have been browbeaten into accepting totally unbiblical behaviour because they really believe they could not or should not do anything about it. These experiences may range from totally unacceptable domestic behaviour to outrageously unbiblical things happening in a local church. They may be irresponsible statements made about a personal tragedy such as illness, accidents or death, or unjust treatment at work or in business.

The only way to avoid these extremes is to understand the difference between this interim period in which we live where the enemy still has certain powers, and the glorious age to come when he will be totally banished forever. Until then we will always be in a struggle. But it is not a hopeless struggle and we must not give in or give up. Rather, we should be aware of the devil's schemes and the power he exerts without being intimidated by it.

The book of Job

The book of Job illustrates the point that the devil wields great power. We need to remember that this book is not primarily about Satan but rather about suffering. More pointedly, it addresses the problem of innocent people suffering. At an even deeper level, it raises the problem of maintaining our faith in God in the face of undeserved and, at least from a human perspective, pointless suffering.

William J Dumbrell puts it succinctly when he says: 'A broader theme broached by Job is the existence of evil in our world and proper reaction to it' (*The Faith of Israel*, p. 218).

Having made that point, we are still left with the fact that Satan seems to be in possession of considerable power on the earth. He appears to have the authority to stir up brigands and terrorists to attack and rob Job (1:15, 17). In addition he seems, at least to some degree, to control wind and lightning to further wreak destruction on Job's possessions (1:16). But we need to be aware of the double play here. In Job 1:11, Satan challenges God Himself to strike Job. God replies to Satan as follows:

> The Lord said to Satan, 'Very well, then, everything he has is in your hands, but on the man himself do not lay a finger.' Then Satan went out from the presence of the Lord. (Job 1:12)

It seems as if divine permission is granted to the adversary to do the harm. Yet in Job 2:3 God maintains that He himself has been incited to act against Job. It implies that in some mysterious way God was behind Job's suffering. This strange statement must not be construed to mean that in some way God's purposes and plans for any of His children can be changed by an argument by any of His creatures, let alone Satan! Rather it must be seen as God allowing His wise and holy purposes to be worked out in Job's life even through the trials of the enemy. We will come back to this point. My concern is merely to remind my readers that Satan at times appears to possess the power to do incalculable harm.

The Gospels and Acts

When we come to the Gospels, we are confronted by a large amount of demonic activity. A demon-possessed man cries out against Jesus in the synagogue (Mark 1:23–24). A demoniac confronts Jesus in the land of the Gerasenes. He is so violent that he has been bound with chains, but to no avail (Luke 8:26–29). A demon causes dumbness in a man (Matthew 9:32–33). A young boy is thrown into violent epileptic fits by demon powers (Matthew 17:14–17). Jesus describes a woman who has been crippled for eighteen years as one 'whom Satan has kept bound' (Luke 13:16).

There was no doubt a great rise in demonic activity during Jesus' day as Satan faced his inevitable defeat at Calvary. Outside the Gospels, only one other incident of demon possession and exorcism is recorded when the apostles were involved (Acts 16:16–18). There is of course the incident involving the seven sons of Sceva (Acts 19:13–16), but in this incident the exorcism was unsuccessful which highlighted the authority the apostles had as opposed to others. The question of apostolic authority was a constant problem. It was a particular problem to Paul and it became an issue he addresses in several of his epistles, notably the epistle to the Galatians.

In all the instances recorded of Christ, the demons were cast out, demonstrating his authority over Satan, demons and the world of the supernatural. But these instances do not illustrate that human lives were deeply affected by the activities of Satan, not only by way of demon possession but in other ways as well. Bearing in mind the experience of Job, we remember the ominous words spoken by Jesus in Luke 22:31–32:

> 'Simon, Simon, Satan has asked to sift you as
> wheat. But I have prayed for you, Simon, that
> your faith may not fail. And when you have
> turned back, strengthen your brothers.'

Here was a request by Satan to test God's servant. In this regard Peter stands as a New Testament counterpart to Job. Peter grievously failed the test, yet unlike his fellow disciple Judas whom Satan entered (John 13:27), Peter did not abandon his faith. He sinned but was restored because Jesus prayed for him. Thus we see a wide range of ways in which Satan has been permitted to harass and afflict human beings on earth. His defeat on Calvary was decisive yet we know that, though defeated, he will continue to wreak havoc until his doom is finally sealed when the Lord Jesus Christ returns from heaven.

No dualism

By dualism I refer to that view of the world that sees the whole of creation in terms of two principles which are independent of each other yet implacably opposed to each other. While there are many ways of using the concept of dualism, I want to emphasise the theological view and make the observation that, while it is true that God is opposed to the devil, we must not make the mistake of setting the devil and God on an equal footing. They are not two equal beings who are striving for ultimate mastery of the world. God is the Creator and in fact created Satan. As Martin Luther said, 'The devil is God's devil'. They are not two equal beings but rather a subordinate created being who rebelled against the Almighty God, the Creator of the universe.

This brings us back to a passage we have already referred to, Job 1:9-12. Although the devil is given permission to afflict Job, the narrative seems to insist that in some way God himself is involved in Job's sufferings. As we saw in the comments of D A Carson quoted earlier, God stands behind both good and evil but not in the same way. All evil can ultimately be traced back to Satan, yet the providential and overruling will of the Almighty God cannot be ruled out. Before Satan can afflict God's people, divine permission must be sought. God permits no suffering or trials without a purpose, even though that purpose may be hidden from us.

How does this affect us in our personal tragedies? What relevance does all this have to, for instance, the victims of the massacre at our church? We must be careful before attributing all disasters and tragedies to the devil. He may certainly be behind some of the things that happen to us as he wages war on the saints. But it is untrue to attribute all the bad things that happen to us to Satan in a willy-nilly manner. This may well give the adversary more power and prominence than he deserves or possesses as well as causing us a great deal of unnecessary stress.

Turning to the Scriptures, we are reminded that illness, for example, is not always from the devil although it can of course be an affliction to tempt us away from God. As noted earlier, Jesus referred to an afflicted woman as bound by Satan. But sickness may equally be from God who, for His own purposes, permits suffering. We have a clear reference to this in Exodus 4:11. In addition, in His love for us, God disciplines us for our sins to bring us to repentance. Miriam's leprosy is an illustration of this (Numbers 12). The psalmist also testifies to this truth in Psalm 119:67, and the apostle Paul affirms this fact in 1 Corinthians 11:30.

A word of great caution needs to be sounded here because in John 9:1–3 we have a clear case of affliction which was brought upon a man purely so that God could be glorified in his healing. The lesson is clear. We must be extremely cautious before attributing all tragedies to the devil in an indiscriminate manner. But we also need to remember that it is possible for the adversary to afflict us with evil. If it is a tragedy of a particularly evil nature such as assault, rape, murder or robbery, we can be sure that such evil belongs to Satan. This does not, of course, excuse the perpetrators in any way. They must be held responsible for their actions. But behind their actions we discern the presence of the evil one, Satan, who seeks constantly to harass the people of God.

It is important to acknowledge that evil things do happen to people who are not Christians too.

In fact evil things often do happen to evil people, even in this life. Behind all evil stands the adversary who through his agents, spiritual as well as human, reflects his evil nature and foists it on society. When these things happen to the children of God, it is sometimes possible to speak of affliction as Satan's attacks.

We must always bear in mind that ultimately our lives are in God's hands. All evil things that happen to us would be entirely impossible without His divine permission. We are not at the mercy of a malevolent devil. Remember, to tempt Peter, he first had to ask for permission!

We must not give in to a mind set that sees a rampaging enemy let loose upon God's people in an uncontrolled manner. We must not think of good and evil as two equal principles battling it out in this world. We must reject this form of dualism. Rather we see God's world, though ruined by sin, still firmly under His control. All things in heaven and earth are His. Even the great adversary is only a created being. He can afflict us or tempt us only with divine permission. He is already doomed and we live in that interim period where he vents his rage in God's world and upon God's work as the dying throes of a doomed creature. We should never take the devil lightly, but on the other hand we should never be intimidated by him.

Revelation 12

No summary of the adversary's activities can be made without referring to the book of Revelation and especially the twelfth chapter. This book was written towards the end of the reign of the emperor Domitian (AD 81–96). Domitian is remembered as an emperor second only to Nero for cruelty. He declared himself *Dominus et Deus Noster*—Our Lord and God—thus bringing to a head the cult of emperor worship. He unleashed vicious persecution on the Christians and was responsible for banning the apostle John to the island of Patmos where John received the vision which we today call the book of Revelation.

The theme of this book is to show us that things are not always what they seem. Often the 'beast'—the force that opposes God—appears to win. But finally he is overthrown by Christ who rules for ever and ever. John Stott sums up the book of Revelation as follows:

The conflict between the church and the

world is seen to be but an expression on the
public stage of the invisible contest between
Christ and Satan, the Lamb and the dragon.
This age-long battle is set forth in a series of
dramatic visions which have been variously
interpreted. (The Cross of Christ, p. 247)

Referring to the various schools of interpretation and
the dramatic images and visions which recur throughout
the book, he offers the following comment which helps
us to understand the book of Revelation:

It seems more probable, therefore, that the
scenes overlap; that the whole history of the
world between Christ's first coming (the victory won) and second (the victory conceded)
is several times recapitulated in vision; and
that the emphasis is on the conflict between
the Lamb and the dragon which has already
had a number of historical manifestations, and
will have more before the End. (Ibid)

Thus we have a series of visions describing the battle
between the church and the world. This in turn represents
the invisible contest between Christ and Satan. It depicts
for us an enemy that struggles futilely against the Lord of
the universe and is finally doomed. Yet in his struggle, he
causes much harm.

Revelation 12 seems to be a summary of the whole book.
It describes a pregnant woman in terms that are meant to
convey great glory. She gives birth to a son who is obviously
the Messiah. A great red dragon appears, grotesque in ap-
pearance, to devour the child. But the child is snatched to
safety. There is a war in heaven and the dragon is hurled to
earth. This is the devil who has been defeated and dethroned.

But his activities have not ended. Powerful conflict continues on a large scale.

Three helpers are introduced to assist this dragon to 'lead the whole world astray' (verse 9). They are two monsters and a 'great prostitute' (17:1). Once again John Stott helps us to understand this vision. He says: 'It becomes evident that all three are symbols of the Roman Empire, although in three different aspects, namely Rome the persecutor, Rome the deceiver and Rome the seducer.' Thus the enemy uses the world, governments and the state to wage war on God's people in different ways—to persecute, to deceive and to seduce. In some countries today the state still opposes God and his church. Christians are persecuted, banished and imprisoned.

But then Jesus the conqueror arrives on a white horse. The last three chapters of Revelation describe his great victory over the dragon and his allies, and the final destruction of Satan and death. The consequences of the fall in the Garden of Eden are ultimately dealt with and a new heaven and earth are ushered in where there is no death, pain or night and all tears are wiped away.

There is no doubt about it: the devil loses in the end. His doom was secured on Calvary and will be finally seen when Christ returns. We who belong to Christ struggle against the enemy knowing that the victory has already been won.

Defeating the devil

How can we appropriate Christ's victory? How can we live in such a way that we will not succumb to the deceits of the adversary? How can we overcome the temptation to abandon our trust in God in the face of suffering and sadness?

In two places in the New Testament we are told to 'resist the devil'. The first is James 4:7:

> Submit yourselves, then, to God. Resist the
> devil, and he will flee from you.

The context is submission to God, purity of life and humility as opposed to pride, slander and censoriousness. The second place is 1 Peter 5:8–9:

> Be self-controlled and alert. Your enemy the
> devil prowls around like a roaring lion looking
> for someone to devour. Resist him, standing
> firm in the faith, because you know that your
> brothers throughout the world are undergo-
> ing the same kind of sufferings.

Once again the context is the deliberate exercise of humility accompanied by a trust in God and a personal watchfulness against the enemy.

I would like to offer the following suggestions to help us in our struggle against the adversary. Firstly, let us adopt a *balanced view of the devil*.

We must not treat him lightly or carelessly. He is a formidable enemy with enormous power to harass the people of God. At the same time we must not lose sight of the fact that his power was decisively broken on the Cross and his doom was irrevocably sealed. We therefore need to be on our guard but not intimidated.

Secondly, *do not be confused by the suffering and tragedy that occurs in this world*. We live in a fallen world. Suffering may come upon us from different sources and for different reasons. We must not become so discouraged that we are tempted, like Job, to curse God. We are not yet in that glorious age when all tears will be wiped away. Rather we are living in that period of time between Satan's overthrow at the cross and his banishment at the final judgement. God, the ruler of the universe, for His own mysterious purpose, still allows the adversary some power to test the faith of his people. We are secure because we are in God's hands, not the devil's.

Thirdly, *beware of blindly and emotionally attributing everything to the devil*. Powerful though the enemy may be, he does not have all power. Only God is all-powerful. Sometimes God himself is at work in our lives to discipline us, sanctify us and help us in our spiritual growth. What we are experiencing may be from him, not the enemy.

Fourthly, let us remember that *the devil is not our only enemy*. We also have to fight the world and the 'flesh', our own natural sinful inclinations. We are sometimes subject to strong temptations and we all have the potential to give in to evil because we are sinners by nature. Although it can be truthfully said that the devil is ultimately behind all sin and evil, we must remember that if we sin, we ourselves choose to do so. We must not blame the devil for our choices. Nor must we blame God for our temptations. We should bear in mind the word of James 1:13–15:

> When tempted, no-one should say, 'God is tempting me.' For God cannot be tempted by evil, nor does He tempt anyone; but each one is tempted when, by his own evil desire, he is dragged away and enticed. Then, after desire has conceived, it gives birth to sin; and sin, when it is full-grown, gives birth to death.

We need to watch ourselves and constantly practise the Christian grace of self-control.

Fifthly, we must bear in mind that *'resisting the devil' does not mean 'rebuking' him by shouting at him*. It refers to a godly lifestyle of submission to God, a break with the friendship of the world and a spirit of personal humility. It means a 'self-watchfullness', setting a guard over ourselves. It is a mind set, an inner desire to live in such a way that we always please God.

This is not the result of an ecstatic or mystical experience but rather the result of God's grace at work in us, giving us an inner desire and determination to honour Him. It is a decision we take in the realm of the will. Effort is required on our part. Paul wrote in 1 Thessalonians 5:6:

> So then, let us not be like others, who are
> asleep, but let us be alert and self-controlled.

We must not be spiritually drowsy or asleep. We should be characterised by an alertness and self-control. We recall that our enemy is like a wild animal, vicious and dangerous. We remember too that we are part of a vast body of people who suffer for Christ. We are therefore not alone and must not be discouraged.

In the sixth place, to resist the enemy *we need to develop the Christian disciplines in our life*. We need to be people of prayer, constantly calling on God for His heavenly grace to defend us. We need to read and understand his Word, for that is where we obtain light, wisdom, understanding and discernment (Psalm 119:130). In prayer before God, we strive for wisdom and we pray that we may be filled with the Holy Spirit daily.

We must refuse to respond to the slightest motions in our heart towards something that is wrong. As believers, our desire should be not to grieve the Holy Spirit. As far as it is possible in this complicated world, we should try to avoid what is obviously wrong and inappropriate behaviour. Thus we strive as part of our Christian discipline to keep up our communion with God.

Then, in the seventh place, *we resolve in our minds that God is God, even when we do not understand His dealings with us.* Tragedy and suffering are part of life in an imperfect world. While we do not sit by passively when it happens, we do not fall into a great state of panic either. Sorrow and grief are the lot of all who live on earth. Shock and sadness may overwhelm us, but sooner or later the children of God find their footing again. We know that, although we can't always see it, all things work together for good to those who love God and are called according to His purpose.

God has a great purpose for His universe and for all His children living in it. We must learn to expect this world and everything in it to 'pass away'. Nothing is permanent. We should learn to hold very lightly to the things of this world, fixing our eyes on the new world where sorrow is banished forever.

In the eighth place, we resist the devil by *refusing to forsake the gospel.* Peter tells us to resist him, 'standing firm in the faith' (1 Peter 5:9). This means that no matter what happens, we refuse to believe that the sorrow or tragedy that overtakes us negates the gospel of the cross, the atonement, forgiveness of our sins and reconciliation with God, his love for us and the glories of the world to come.

'Does Job fear God for nothing?' was the question Satan put to God. 'But stretch out your hand and strike everything he has, and he will surely curse you to your face' (Job 1:9, 11). In other words, the great temptation that accompanies trials and tragedies is to curse God, to reject Him and forsake Him. But not so for true Christians. Just as Job maintained his integrity, so should we. 'Though He slay me, yet will I hope in Him,' said Job (13:15). The same must be true for us.

We may not understand, we may be hurt and confused, but we refuse to believe the lies whispered by the Evil One during days of suffering. We refuse to forsake the gospel.

We stand firm in the faith. We will not give up one inch of gospel territory. We believe it all, even when God seems far away from us, until He brings the sunshine into our lives again.

Finally, we remember that to resist the devil includes the need to *proclaim the gospel*. The kingdom of darkness retreats before the kingdom of light. We must continue to witness to the truth of the Bible and the gospel of the cross that it proclaims. As we do so, people will understand more fully the great work of Christ on the cross and that the enemy has been defeated. They themselves will be lifted from darkness to light and from despair to joy. And as we place ourselves constantly under the sound of God's Word, so our own understanding will increase and we will receive inner strength to carry the burdens God may place upon us.

Conclusion

As we struggle with the suffering and tragedy of life, sooner or later the role of the devil will come up. While we recognise the great power he wields in the world, and that indeed he may have had a hand in our present suffering, we are not intimidated. We remember that even Satan is under the control of God and that he can do nothing without divine permission. Thus although Satan is responsible for all sin and evil, we also know that our sovereign and loving heavenly Father is with us in all our sufferings.

We remember too that our Lord's death on the cross was the decisive defeat of Satan. He no longer has the power of fear and death over us. We may need to put up with his harassment, but we learn to resist him by a godly lifestyle, a determination to obey God and by walking humbly. We are watchful in all we do and we know that as we resist him in this way, accompanied by prayer to God and a personal walk with Him, the enemy will flee from us.

No doubt the devil was involved in the massacre in our church. Death and destruction, hatred and violence are his trademark. But no, he did not win the day. God in his great mercy used the occasion to draw near to His suffering people with an abundant measure of His presence, thus proving His promises to be true. He overruled the evil one by drawing hundreds of people to Himself. He gave the gospel a prominence and an acceptability, even if momentarily, that it has seldom had in this country.

Let us close this chapter with some words from Martin Luther's great hymn 'A Mighty Fortress':

> And though this world with devils filled
> Should threaten to undo us
> We will not fear, for God has willed
> His truth to triumph through us
> The prince of darkness grim
> We tremble not for him
> His rage we can endure
> For lo! his doom is sure
> One little word shall fell him.
>   (Great Hymns of the Faith)

9

Lessons We Learn from Suffering and Tragedy

I want to summarise the ground we have covered so far and attempt to draw together some of the strands that have run through this book to help us identify the lessons we learn from suffering and tragedy. I am well aware that all forms of suffering have lessons to teach us and that in essence all suffering and tragedy basically underscores the same lessons. But I am also aware that different people will learn different things from life's events. We are not always impressed with the observations other people make. Sometimes our own observations appear far more pertinent. Yet there are observations that need to be made and that have wide application to us all.

Trials are unavoidable

We must do away once and for all with the great myth that suffering is never part of God's will. Besides the fact that this is simply not true and is clearly not supported by Scripture, this teaching is cruel and destructive. Ask any minister or counsellor and they are sure to be able to recount instances of people who have been deeply hurt by this teaching.

People are sometimes told that their suffering or misfortune is due either to lack of faith or some sin of which they need to repent. We have often had to help people who have been emotionally battered by others who have told them that their problems have been caused by demons. You can imagine what an assertion like that may mean to a sensitive person struggling with a problem but not knowledgeable enough to counteract this kind of spiritual abuse.

I do not mean to suggest that personal sin in our lives does not bring the fruit of trouble and bitterness. Nor do I mean to imply that Christians do not have problems with Satan, our archenemy. On the contrary, we most certainly do. That is why the apostle Peter tells us to resist him (1 Peter 5:8–9). He is likened to a fierce and ravenous wild animal who seeks to destroy us.

I most certainly do not want to denigrate any attempt made to fight the enemy or to fight the sinfulness of our human hearts. But I do most sincerely want to raise a voice against the unthinking and unbiblical actions of some people which cause a great deal of hurt to others who are already hurting because those ministering to them are basing their actions on the myth that suffering is never God's will.

The Monday morning after the Sunday night attack on our church was the worst Monday morning of my life. I had finally fallen into a fitful sleep in the early hours and woke early with a pounding heart. I dreaded the thought of getting dressed and going back to the church. I knew the media would be there in force. I knew too that the police would be on the site. I did not want to go back into the building itself. I did not know what to say to those who were bereaved. Furthermore, I dreaded the news from the hospitals. Our monitors would all be busy and information would be fed to me throughout the day.

The day was as dreadful as I had anticipated. News conferences, individual media people, international linkups, police, faxes, ringing telephones, multitudes of messages and immediate decisions became a blur in my memory.

The last major event on that Monday was a programme on South African TV. It was a news programme which presented background to the day's events. Because it was a live broadcast arranged at the last minute, there would be no opportunity to go over the questions as was usually possible for participants. I had no idea what I would be asked and I had a thumping headache which had never lifted from my jet lag of the day before.

God enabled me to acquit myself well on the programme but the tension of the day had taken its toll. I returned home utterly fatigued and feeling incredibly sad in my spirit. Late that night as I was preparing for bed, the phone rang. It was a woman who was a complete stranger to me. I thought at first that she was one of the multitudes of callers who phoned to express concern, prayer support and Christian solidarity.

It may help to point out at this juncture that my church is not part of the charismatic or pentecostal tradition within evangelicalism. I also want to say that while our views on these things are well-known in Cape Town, there is nevertheless a warm sense of fraternal fellowship and respect between charismatic and pentecostal pastors and myself. Many of these dear brothers were among the first to express their grief and support at the time.

I greeted the late-night caller warmly if a little wearily. Instead of the assurance of prayer such as those which had flooded in all day, she informed me that she knew why this thing had happened in our church. 'Oh?' I queried. 'Please explain, because I myself would like to know.'

I knew what she was going to say. It was because I neglected the Holy Spirit in my teaching and did not lead my congregation into the experience of tongues and the ecstatic gifts of the Spirit. It was my fault that this tragedy had occurred and what I needed to do was to repent.

The last thing I needed that Monday night was this kind of call. I thank God that through the years I have had to think through these issues and, rather than being upset at her accusations, I wondered at the utter insensitivity and arrogance of this person who felt she was uniquely filled with the Holy Spirit yet was unable in any way to discern the pain and burden I was enduring that night.

A letter that came from a pentecostal pastor in England some days later contained the same rebuking message and warned me that God was telling me to 'get into pentecost'. I must hasten to add that these two individuals do not represent the enormous support, love and prayers showered on us by the charismatic and pentecostal communities in Cape Town and around the country. However, it does portray the kind of thinking I am trying to illustrate. This mentality is rooted in the understanding that if you are doing the right things and observing all the right 'rituals' (baptism of the Spirit, tongues speaking, etc), suffering is not part of God's will for you. But biblical evidence contradicts this. Not only is there evidence that people who honour God do suffer, there are also references to the additional fact that God Himself sometimes stands behind these sufferings and, for His own inscrutable purpose, does not alleviate them even though He has the power to do so. We need turn no further than Exodus 4 for an illustration. In his excellent book 'When God Doesn't Make Sense', Dr James Dobson makes the following comment about this passage:

> You'll also remember the story of Moses and his encounter with the voice of God in the burning bush (Exodus 3–4). The Lord in-

structed him to confront Pharaoh and demand that the children of Israel be released from Egyptian captivity. When Moses asked why the children of Israel should believe God had sent him, the Lord armed him with miraculous powers. He turned his staff into a snake and back again into a staff. Then He caused Moses' hand to become leprous and made it healthy again. Finally, God told him that if they would not believe those two signs, he should take water from the Nile River and pour it on the ground and it would turn into blood. These startling feats were designed to reveal the power of God and to authenticate Moses as His representative.

But then a curious thing happened. Moses complained that he lacked eloquence for the task—'I am slow of speech and tongue' (Exodus 4:10)—yet the Lord did not offer to heal that infirmity. Doesn't that seem strange? He had just performed uncanny miracles that enabled Moses to carry out His mission. Why wouldn't He eliminate this troublesome speech impediment? He certainly had the power to do so. Wouldn't it have been logical for the Lord to have said, 'You're going to need a strong voice to lead a million people through the wilderness. Henceforth, you will speak with authority!' No, that isn't the way Jehovah responded. First, He became angry at Moses for using this source of weakness as an excuse. Then He designated Aaron, Moses' brother, to serve as his mouthpiece. Why didn't He just 'do the job right' and get rid of the problem? We don't know. As I've said before, there are times when

God doesn't make sense.

We can assume that the Lord didn't heal Moses' 'slowness of tongue' because Moses, like Paul, was learning that his strength was made perfect in weakness. He was chosen for leadership not because he was a miracle-worker or a superman but because the Lord determined to use his inadequacies and shortcomings. (When God Doesn't Make Sense, pp. 103–104)

In fact God makes a most intriguing statement to Moses:

The Lord said to him, 'Who gave man his mouth? Who makes him deaf or mute? Who gives him sight or makes him blind? Is it not I, the Lord?'

(Exodus 4:11)

Don't you find it amazing that in the face of so many 'healers' who claim that deafness, dumbness and blindness is from the devil, God Himself should claim responsibility for these conditions? Of course we must balance these comments by asserting that God's children have every right to take their ailments, sufferings and circumstances to their heavenly Father. More than that, they should look to Him for His divine intervention. Yet at the same time they need to be careful not to claim things from God that He has not promised. Among the many other biblical examples that could be used to show that sometimes suffering is in fact part of God's will for us, I refer to Hebrews 11. This famous chapter that lists some of the heroes of faith includes those who were 'tortured and refused to be released' (verse 35) and then follow these words:

Some faced jeers and flogging, while still others were chained and put in prison. They were stoned; they were sawn in two; they were put to death by the sword. They went about in sheepskins and goatskins, destitute, persecuted and ill-treated—the world was not worthy of them. They wandered in deserts and mountains, and in caves and holes in the ground.

(Hebrews 11:36-38)

Is this not a list of sufferings? These were people of faith who lived in obedience to God, yet they were called upon to endure suffering in this way. We can be sure that there are times when trials must be faced and true faith must be displayed. These things are unavoidable.

Unexplained suffering

Probably one of the hardest aspects of suffering to endure is the fact that our suffering is not explained. It would be so much easier if we knew why. As I pointed out in Chapter four, there are certain things we can discern in times of trial, but often the immediate cause of suffering is hidden from us.

The problem is that we feel there must always be an understandable reason for everything that happens. Let me illustrate this from another area of life's sorrows—the break-up of a marriage. So often I have to face the anguished cry of a betrayed spouse who has discovered a partner's affair and been devastated by the pending break-up of a marriage. The usual cry is: 'What did I do?' I have often been amazed to observe in these circumstances how the innocent person takes the blame for the actions of the erring spouse. This is often followed by days of frantic heart-searching and finally the person alights on an imagined or real fault. 'That's it!' the wounded partner exclaims. 'If I can only put *that* right the marriage will come together again.'

Unfortunately it does not. So often I have had the unpleasant task of telling a weeping wife that her husband is doing what he is doing because he wants to do it. Period. There need be no other reason. I am not discounting the multifaceted causes for marital breakdown in our modern society. Rather I am trying to focus on the instinct we have to rationalise our disasters. We need to put them into a framework so that we can cope emotionally. Therefore when tragedy strikes on a wider level in our lives, we feel the urgent need to ask God 'Why?' The problem is that we usually get no answer.

In Chapter three I mentioned the problem of the seeming contradiction between the existence of God and the existence of evil, and that sooner or later we have to face the fact that God's dealings with us are often inscrutable. We will not always understand or be given a specific answer. From the Scriptures we can trace God's general purposes in permitting suffering, but we are often left in the dark when it comes to the actual tragedy we are facing.

For instance, Job did not know what was happening when his world crashed around him. Nor did Mary and Martha understand why their brother was allowed to die when they had sent a message to Jesus that he was ill (John 11). They could see no purpose in it. They were not spared the experience of grief, sorrow or tears. But as we know now, there was a purpose in it. Lazarus was to become a symbol of the new life that Jesus imparts to all who believe in Him. But they did not know that at the time.

Unless we come to terms with the inscrutability of God, we will continue to live in doubt, bitterness and self-pity. It is possible to harbour anger towards God for years and waste our lives. We can shut ourselves off from Him, if we choose to, but ultimately we are the loser. Far better to acknowledge humbly that there are times when His ways are hidden from us and that we do not understand all things. We know that God is good and therefore we must come to the place where we cast ourselves unreservedly on the attributes of His character. We take comfort from what we know about Him. And what we can know about Him is so great and glorious that we can confidently trust what we do not know about Him. Our God is a good God.

Trials test our faith

Scripture teaches plainly and clearly that trials test our faith. There is no mystery here.

> Consider it pure joy, my brothers, whenever you face trials of many kinds, because you know that the testing of your faith develops perseverance.
>
> (James 1:2–3)

> In this you greatly rejoice, though now for a little while you may have had to suffer grief in all kinds of trials. These have come so that your faith—of greater worth than gold, which perishes even though refined by fire—may be proved genuine and may result in praise, glory and honour when Jesus Christ is revealed.
>
> (1 Peter 1:6–7)

Before I answer the question why faith is tested, let

me make the point that the faith spoken of here is not vague and undefined. It is quite fashionable today to believe in something; for some people faith appears nothing more than a vague belief in yourself or a force or positive mind set that makes you believe that everything will work out somehow.

Biblical faith is very different. It is not rooted in ourselves. Rather, it is placed in the person of Jesus Christ and all He accomplished by His death and resurrection. It is a total embracing of the gospel with all its implications for living in this world. It is a living connection with God through Jesus Christ our Lord.

True faith saves us. It enables the wonderful benefits of our Lord's suffering on the cross to become ours. It prepares us for eternity and bestows on us the inestimable gift of eternal life. It is no wonder that the apostle Peter describes this faith as 'of greater worth than gold' (1 Peter 1:7). What can possibly take its place that will bring us its benefits?

If this is so, why must this faith be tested? For the simple reason that not all faith is true saving faith. Apart from the meaningless vagueness that some people describe as faith, it is entirely possible for others to be religiously deluded. In our Lord's time there were people who really thought that they were accepted by God on the basis of their ancestry from Abraham (John 8:31–47). Our Lord was very candid in telling them that, far from being the children of God, they were in fact slaves to sin and children of the devil. Their faith was false.

Even today people assume that they are Christians simply because of a church connection or because some ritual has been observed. One of the great difficulties in trying to show people their need of the Saviour is the fact that so many are 'cultural Christians'. By this I mean that for many in the Western world their lives have somehow included the church. Going to church on certain occasions is part of the culture. All the important events of life are celebrated in the church—weddings, the baptism or dedication of babies, the confirmation of children and the burial of the dead. If you asked them whether they are Christians, they would say yes. So true faith has to be tested.

How is the world ever to know what true faith is if it is not displayed in some way? True faith in Christ is not seen too clearly when everything goes well. When there are no difficulties, it is easy for people to claim to be Christians. But when the pressures come, it is an entirely different story. What a man really believes is seen when the chips are down. What is in the head comes out when there is nothing external to lean on. True Christians do not respond to the trials of life in the same way that non-Christians do. Thus true faith is demonstrated most clearly in times of suffering.

I am not suggesting that only Christians have courage. Far from it. I have known people who had no faith in Christ to face adversity with tremendous courage. Being unafraid to die is something that is not limited to Christians. It is not raw courage we are talking about here, for many people of differing persuasions can demonstrate courage. No, it is faith in Christ, the interpreting of life's events, the knowledge that a divine plan is being worked out that needs to be seen. It is the freedom from the fear that we live in a random and meaningless universe; it is the deep assurance that even in the midst of the worst life can offer us, we are still a loved people. It is a sense of peace and purpose that goes beyond the norm of daily experience. It is the deep conviction that this life is not all there is but that beyond the boundaries set by our three score years and ten, there is another world.

In the aftermath of our tragedy we found the evidence of true faith overwhelming. The thing that struck me is that true faith in Christ , as opposed to that which is false, has a ring of truth about it. It is not acted out. Rather it is a spontaneous response of the heart. The humble heart-warming response of so many of our church members during those days brought tears to my eyes.

And true faith does indeed go on display. During those days we were very much aware that the eyes of the nation were on us. We received scores of letters telling us how the display of true faith gave other individuals or church groups courage to go on witnessing for Christ. In His own wonderful way, God took the trials of our church and the display of faith it produced to affirm the faith of countless other Christians around the country.

God is with us in our sufferings

Something that we learned that is very difficult to express is the fact that in times of great trial and tragedy, God truly stands by His people. This is no less than He promised. Take the words of Jesus in John 14:27:

> Peace I leave with you; my peace I give you.
> I do not give to you as the world gives. Do
> not let your hearts be troubled and do not
> be afraid.

How can I ever convey to you the experience of that night and the days that followed? Surely, he gave us His peace. In the midst of all the horror of that evening, a peculiar calm descended on our congregation. The police commented afterwards that they had never seen anything like it. Usually in times of violence or disaster there is a mass stampede for the exit. There was however no mind-less panic on the night. The congregation left the church quietly and in an orderly fashion. While some rushed away from the scene, hundreds stayed to assist with the injured and with police enquiries. Many people rose to the occasion in a special way and helped the injured with calmness and purpose.

Something supernatural occurred at that time. The newspapers speculated that people might not want to come back to the church. Yet our services have been more than packed since. Many people told me that they decided to become members of our church after the massacre took place. The bereaved, though hurting and grieving, nevertheless experienced abundant measures of God's grace. As I am writing this, I realise afresh how futile it is to try to describe what happened. I cannot put into words the fresh sense of peace, power and assurance that enveloped us.

I know that Christians often testify to the sense of God's peace. And it is true that we do enjoy His presence under normal circumstances. But there is a measure of His presence which is reserved for His people when they go through terrible trial and suffering. In Daniel 3 we have the wonderful account of Shadrach, Meshach and Abednego, the three Israelites who refused to bow to an image of King Nebuchadnezzar. As a result they were thrown into the fiery furnace. They made their famous defiant and confident reply to the king:

> Shadrach, Meshach and Abednego replied to the king, 'Our Nebuchadnezzar, we do not need to defend ourselves before you in this matter. If we are thrown into the blazing furnace, the God we serve is able to save us from it, and He will rescue us from your hand, Our king. But even if He does not, we want you to know, Our king, that we will not serve

your gods or worship the image of gold you
have set up.'

(Daniel 3:16–18)

Then follows the amazing account of what happened
in the fiery furnace:

Then King Nebuchadnezzar leaped to his feet
in amazement and asked his advisers, 'Weren't
there three men that we tied up and threw
into the fire?' They replied, 'Certainly, O
king.' He said. 'Look! I see four men walking around in the fire, unbound and unharmed, and the fourth looks like a son of
the gods.'

(Daniel 3:24–25)

The presence of the fourth man was a special experience during their fiery ordeal. They did not have that kind
of experience in the normal course of events. Yet when
they needed Him, He was there. So it was with us. The
fourth man walked among us in those days and we were
not burned. And why should you not also experience his
grace and presence during your trial? Let me return to
Isaiah 43:2 where we read:

When you pass through the waters,
I will be with you;
and when you pass through the rivers,
they will not sweep over you.
When you walk through the fire,
you will not be burned;
the flames will not set you ablaze.

The words 'I will be with you' indicate God's presence with His people in a unique way. But it was reserved for 'when you pass through the waters'. Left to us, we would want that special and unique grace all the time. But that special grace is for special occasions. You can speak to any Christian you know who has been through deep waters. They will tell you the same story. God was with them. His peace upheld them. His everlasting arms were underneath them. Everything we ever believed about God standing by His people in times of suffering was proved true.

I often wondered during those days what people do who do not have Christ as their Saviour. Where do they go? To whom do they turn when disaster comes upon them? I recall a sad instance many years ago when I tried to minister to an elderly couple in deep trouble. She was dying of cancer and desperately wanted to talk about spiritual matters. He saw the church as a threat. Their entire lives had been lived in blatant defiance of God.

Suddenly they were no longer in control of their lives. The man's whole frame of reference had been shaken and his pathetic reaction was to 'protect' his wife from the church. She had something on her mind about which she obviously wanted to talk. On the one occasion I had of speaking with her, she kept repeating one question over and over: 'Will He forgive me? Will He forgive me?' She could not grasp the gospel and I was given no more time with her. As far as I know, she went to the grave with that question on her lips: 'Will He forgive me?' She had lived for the world and in her darkest moment, the world had nothing to offer her.

'I do not give [peace] to you as the world gives,' said Jesus (John 14:27). How blessedly true that is.

Reordered priorities

Sudden tragedy has a way of bringing life into sharp focus. The horror of sudden death that night made people take stock of their priorities. Life seemed to fall into perspective. When life loses its predictability and shows us how uncertain it is, the petty things are seen for what they are—petty.

Family suddenly became terribly important. Wives and husbands found each other in a new way that evening. The little conflicts and arguments which may have been part of their lives together were suddenly thrown out of the window. As the terrible losses to some members of the congregation emerged, so a deep gratitude developed that they themselves had been spared. And as the picture became clearer of the maiming and the injuries, people shuddered to think what might have been.

We were all so grateful that the scores of small children had been removed from the church before the attackers appeared. A special children's programme had been prepared across the campus in the Children's Centre. After the attack, the children panicked. Yet because the workers on the children's team that night did not know what was happening, they kept the children locked in the centre. When parents and children were finally reunited, the moment was too emotional to describe.

You may discover in your own circumstances how important loved ones are. We sometimes go through life taking our loved ones for granted. Then suddenly we nearly lose them and we see them with new eyes. We all saw that time was too short and life too uncertain to waste on the trivialities that cause tension. We need to make every moment count.

The same applied to friendships. It is a fact of life that many people remain single. For the single people in our church, that night was a time of fresh bonding. Loved ones and friends came to the church with shock on their faces to enquire after relatives and friends. Indescribable relief flooded over them as they found their friends unharmed. Sadness and shock took hold of others as they were told of loved ones who had been injured. How important friends became.

There was a new sense of bonding in the congregation. Not only among family and friends, but in the church family as a whole. I've never been so hugged in all my life. People hugged each other simply out of spontaneous gratitude to be alive and able to enjoy each other's company. Bonding in suffering is a special kind of bonding. It is known by those who go to war or who suffer some disaster together. But the faith of Christian fellowship adds a dimension that is difficult to define.

Overlapping problems

One of the important lessons learned during this period was the possibility of having to face more than one problem. People caught up in sudden disaster and suffering often bring into that suffering a host of other problems.

In our church we have a regular stream of visitors and newcomers brought by friends and relatives. Many of the people in the service on the night of the attack had unresolved problems in their lives. It may have been a marriage problem or a job problem. It may have been a health problem that was causing fear and uncertainty. Then the disaster struck. Immediately the shock and horror dwarfed everything else, but when we began our debriefing programmes, we discovered that the traumatic effect of the attack on the church had been added to other existing problems.

The person concerned may have suffered from deep shock and severe depression. They did not realise that they were in fact struggling with two distinct problems. For instance the depression that descended on them after the attack had become merged with the depression they were experiencing because their marriage was disintegrating. It was all jumbled up in their minds and for a long time they were unable to separate the issues.

You may experience something similar in your own life. It is perfectly possible for us to carry heavy burdens and to feel downcast without being able to pinpoint the cause. Often our difficulty lies in the fact that we are actually dealing with more than one problem and each difficulty needs to be resolved separately. A debriefing session or a counselling session may be helpful in relation to the post-traumatic stress of the actual tragedy, but if there are other unresolved issues in your life, the feelings of depression, aimlessness, sadness and irritability won't go away. We need help to analyse our situation, distinguish between the different problems and seek biblical solutions for them.

Evangelism

Isn't it strange how predictable we are? If a group of Christian leaders had been asked to devise a plan to reach our nation with the gospel, no doubt they would have thought of inviting someone like Billy Graham to South Africa to conduct huge televised gospel campaigns. But God's plan to touch our nation was to take a church, subject it to tragedy, and display it to the nation. The results have been significant. More than 350 people responded to the gospel invitation at the funeral services alone. In addition we have had a steady stream of enquirers after our church services since the massacre. We have had people walking off the streets and knocking on our church office door, asking for help to find God. In addition, from all around the country, we have had reports of thousands of Christians who have had opportunities of witnessing to their faith that they would not normally have had. Many reported the spontaneous way colleagues at work or members of their family turned to them to open discussions about the things they believed. Many churches reported increased attendances after the massacre as thousands of Christians responded to the crisis. Unbelievers sought out their churches, seeking answers, and many faithful preachers had new opportunities to sow the good seed of the gospel as well as to reap a harvest for eternity.

An unexpected bonus in terms of evangelism was the media. I was constantly being interviewed, and in fact for weeks afterwards, people commented on things they had heard me say in a programme or read in a newspaper or magazine. At the time of writing, the issue is still very much alive in South Africa. Because of the horrendous injuries inflicted on one of the Ukrainian seamen, Dimitri Makagon, there are constant follow-up stories. The fact that his young fiancée, Olga, has flown to be at his bedside has added a strong romantic human-interest dimension to the story which helps to keep it alive. The longer it remains alive, the longer people remain open to the gospel.

Dimitri and Olga appeared in church again three months after the incident. They received a long standing ovation from the packed congregation. At that moment, memories were relived. Many people wept openly and yet another step in bonding and healing took place. But more than that, even the hardest heart in the building had to melt at the symbolism of the occasion. Here were two young people far from home. They had never been exposed to an evangelical church before. The most horrendous injuries had been inflicted on Dimitri . Yet, without bitterness, he was back in the very place where it all happened. In the swirling cauldron of South African politics, it is not uncommon to hear even churchmen calling for mass action and revenge. The reaction of this couple as well as the rest of the congregation stands in sharp contrast to those whose view of the gospel is different to ours.

Amazing conversions have taken place. A fireman on duty that night could not get the picture of the carnage out of his mind. He phoned later to say that he had been so moved that he had given his life to Christ. A hardened newspaper reporter was so moved by what he saw that he decided to come to the funeral in his private capacity. There he indicated his need of the Saviour. When our follow-up visitation team called on him, he gladly surrendered to Christ. Then there were the police who could not understand the kindness with which they were treated. The police are so often vilified in South African society that this was a new experience for them. Quietly, some of them found a place in the pews on the succeeding Sundays.

In all tragedy and suffering there is the possibility of holding out hope for others. People are more ready to talk when life seems uncertain. In your own set of circumstances, God may have used you to speak up for the gospel or to reflect Christ. Never underestimate the evangelistic potential of suffering.

Putting wrong things right

A further lesson we learned during this time was that we all have a limited time to put wrong things right. As I mentioned, petty things looked very stupid that night. We began to urge each other not to waste time. It's a good lesson for us all to learn.

Is there a letter that you know you have to write? Then

do it now. Is there a phone call you must make? Then do it now. Is there a relationship that must be put right, a decision that must be revised? Then do it now. Life is too short and uncertain to procrastinate. If you have something to give away, then do so now. Have the joy of seeing what it means to the other person to receive what it is you want to give. Don't hang on to material things if they can benefit others.

Now is the time to let go of bitterness and silly quarrels. There was a couple who had a family quarrel. They had barely spoken to each other that weekend. On Sunday afternoon they saw how silly it all was and, holding each other in their arms, they apologised and affirmed their love for each other. That night they came to church, as was their custom. He was killed instantly in the attack. How grateful his wife was that their last afternoon together was one of tenderness and affirmation.

Now is the time to reach out to someone who needs to hear you say, 'I'm sorry.' Do not let disaster overtake you and rob you of the challenge of putting things right for the sake of Jesus Christ.

Personal penitence

In our own experience we faced the days that followed filled with a sense of personal heart-searching. As people came back with friends to show them where they had been sitting, they noticed a bullet hole through the back of the pew right next to where they had sat. As they realised how close they had come to dying or being injured, a new solemnity came upon them. They asked the question 'What if it had been me?' Many realised that they were not real Christians at all. Others were faced with the fact that their spiritual lives had been rather shabby. There was

a deep sense of heart-searching and personal seeking of
God and his grace. But there was more. Some people realised how important it was for their loved ones to have a
right relationship with God. Restraints were lifted and
those who were in the building that night were openly
and lovingly challenged by others. 'Are you right with
God?' they were asked. Many faced the question : 'Where
would you have gone if it was you who had been killed?'

You may think such questions are a little crude and
perhaps even unfeeling. But in a time of tragedy when
death flashed suddenly out of the shadows, larger priorities than tender sensitivities came into focus. Eternal issues loomed large and the reality that we are all heading
for an eternal destiny took hold of people. Questions such
as these appeared entirely in place and normal. There was
nothing strained or artificial about them. In fact people
were more than willing to answer them or to get help in
thinking them through.

Listening ears

Let me close this section by remarking on the new
spirit that came into the congregation at our public gath-
erings. As the following Sunday arrived, I was exhausted.
My greatly respected colleague Ross Anderson, who shares
the preaching load with me, was equally exhausted. He
was leading the service on the night of the attack. Miraculously, he was unhurt and was able—quite magnificently—
to keep some order from the platform during the ensuing
confusion. But he too was utterly drained. What were we
to say to these people?

We decided on a series of sermons entitled 'The Road

to Recovery'. It was simple, basic and we tried to be biblical and encouraging. We were utterly staggered by the response of the people. They listened with an urgency I have never seen before. Instead of settling back in their pews as people do when the sermon begins, they leaned forward. There was a deadly earnestness about it all. It was as if the nearness of eternity triggered something off in their hearts. Oh, how they listened. It made me think of our Lord's words in Luke 8:18: 'Therefore consider carefully how you listen.' People literally hung on our words.

It was also a reflection of the new note of urgency in our preaching. We were preaching for eternity. Yes, we were seeking to help a wounded and traumatised congregation. But more than that, we realised in a new way that we were preaching to people who would die someday. And hundreds of new people were coming to our services. They were confused, frightened, curious, hungry and, above all, wide open to hear of Christ and his saving death on the cross. It was a time of great opportunity and somehow by God's grace we summoned hidden reserves of energy to preach as 'dying men to dying men'.

What days they were as service by service people responded to the gospel. We invited them to respond by coming to us after the service and requesting an evangelistic booklet we had offered. Within the first three months after the event, more than a thousand people took up the offer.

Tragedy and suffering is a time for God to speak. He speaks through us and he speaks to us. It is a time when we need to do personal heart-searching. It is a time to take stock of where we are going with our lives. Are we true Christians or not? Are we living as true disciples of Christ or not? Is there a spiritual integrity in our lives?

10

A Way Forward

Henry Vaughan wrote the following words in the hymn 'Religion':

> Heal then these waters, Lord: or bring Thy
> flock
> since these are troubled, to the springing
> rock,
> look down great Master of the feast; O shine,
> and turn once more our water into wine!

Is it possible that God will turn once again the water of adversity and affliction into the wine of joy and peace for us? The answer must be affirmative. Not only is the Bible full of great promises from God to the people who belong to Him; it is also full of examples of our God turning the fortunes of those who are abused, sinned against, betrayed, hurt and wrongly judged. They emerge from the shadows into the sunshine of His smile. We only have to mention the names of people like Abraham, Jacob, Job, David and Daniel to make the point.

In the New Testament we follow the failures of the disciples and the trials of the apostles with great interest. Beaten, abused, rejected—still they were filled with joy, loved by many and accomplished great things for God. They stand as examples for us. God can and does 'turn our water into wine'.

In his excellent commentary on the book of Job, David Atkinson puts it this way:

Suffering will end: but when, we do not know. But we do know that the Lord will come, and He will transform our 'wounds into worships'. That is the word of hope from Job for people who are waiting with anxiety and uncertainty—wondering, maybe, where God is in their lives. The Lord will come! In the death of Christ, on the cross of Calvary, we are shown the lengths to which God's love will come. And in the cross we see not only the suffering of the crucified God, our Kinsman-Redeemer; we see the gift of new life and hope secured. 'He has borne our griefs and carried our sorrows.'

We are not promised freedom from suffering in this world. 'In the world you will have tribulation.' Nor are we let into all of God's secrets. But we are promised grace. For some, there may be healing and restoration in this life. For others, that gift awaits them in the 'new heavens and the new earth' where there will be no more pain, no more tears, no more death. But for all of us, here and how, there is grace, and there can be hope. (The Message of Job, p. 162)

These are fine sounding words, but how do we actually get our lives together again after tragedy and suffering? Are there any guidelines? I would like to share six principles with you as I end this book. I believe they form a healthy set of practical rules for the future. They are drawn from Ecclesiastes 11:1–6 Two books that I have used extensively in this section are Matthew Poole's *Commentary on the Holy Bible* and *The Message of Ecclesiastes* by Derek Kidner:

Cast your bread upon the waters,
for after many days you will find it again.
Give portions to seven, yes to eight,
for you do not know what disaster
may come upon the land.
If clouds are full of water,
they pour rain upon the earth.
Whether a tree falls to the south or to the
        north,
in the place where it falls, there will it lie.
Whoever watches the wind will not plant;
whoever looks at the clouds will not reap.
As you do not know the path of the wind,
or how the body is formed in a mother's
        womb,
so you cannot understand the work of God,
the Maker of all things.
Sow your seed in the morning,
and at evening let not your hands be idle,
for you do not know which will succeed,
whether this or that,
or whether both will do equally well.

The element of risk

Cast your bread upon the waters,
for after many days you will find it again.
                              (Ecclesiastes 11:1)

In this verse the word 'bread' probably stands for one's
trade or livelihood and the word 'cast' should be trans-
lated 'send'. This probably refers to trading by sea which
was a much greater risk in those days than it is today. In
other words, just because life is uncertain it doesn't mean

that we should sit down and do nothing. Get on with the business of life and living. We cannot control the world nor can we anticipate everything that might happen. Life is very unpredictable. The normal rules do not always seem to apply as the following quotation, also from Ecclesiastes, illustrates:

> I have seen something else under the sun:
> The race is not to the swift
> or the battle to the strong,
> nor does food come to the wise
> or wealth to the brilliant
> or favour to the learned;
> but time and chance happen to them all.
> (Ecclesiastes 9:11)

We can be paralysed by fear after a traumatic event as we witnessed in our own situation. After the event there were several people who were too scared to venture out. Life can appear so utterly overwhelming that we may be too scared to move. But sooner or later we have to make the choice of getting on with our lives. We can never create a situation about us that is risk free. Life is full of risks.

The writer of Ecclesiastes knew this truth. Yet he urged his readers not to be intimidated by risks. Get back into business. Ply your trade across the seas. 'After many days you will find it again.' In other words, you may be surprised at the result. The risk may be worth it after all.

Many who go through the trauma of a marriage break-up feel that they will never recover. If the break-up was caused by an unsuspected affair with a third person and a subsequent walkout, the sense of loss and trauma is enormous. The sense of hurt and loss is deepened by a sense of betrayal and thoughts about the spouse with the other person. Often the depression resulting from this is so deep the injured party feels suicidal. But the truth is that there is hope; people do survive the traumas of life. God has graciously built into us a resistance that enables us to fight back and pick up the pieces. So much so that, in spite of being hurt and betrayed, people who have suffered in this way will quite often remarry. If their first experience of marriage was so disastrous, why do they go through with a second marriage? All other considerations aside, there is a realisation within us all that life cannot be lived without risks. We have to make the choice to get back on track and live as normal a life as possible.

This truth was illustrated recently by a horrific report in our newspapers of a teenage girl who was brutally assaulted and raped by her own father. She suffered severe trauma but with the help and support of family, her psychiatrist and the state prosecutor, she slowly overcame the tendencies to suicide and the feelings of utter worthlessness and humiliation. Eventually she was not only strong enough to talk about it to the press, but was also willing to name her father publicly and face him in court (Weekend Argus, 30 October 1993).

The point I want to make is that it is possible to recover from sadness and tragedy. Life does indeed go on and we have to make choices about who and what is going to control us.

I am not trying to minimise the effect of tragedy, nor am I suggesting that everyone succeeds in coping with the aftermath. Clearly, some people do not. But if people who are not Christians are able to summon the inner resources to go on with life, how much more those of us who have a living relationship with Christ. We have the resource of prayer and access into God's presence. We can go into the throne room and obtain, by His grace, the strength to go on.

There is no such thing as a life free of risk. We take a

risk in all we do. When we choose a marriage partner and exchange vows, we take a risk. We believe that our partner will keep their vows. But what if they don't? That is the risk we take. In friendships in which confidences are exchanged, we take the risk that those friendships and confidences will be honoured. What else can we do? We can only place our lives in the hands of the living God and launch into life, honestly believing that our destiny is in His hands.

We need not live with fear any longer. Remember that Christ is the Good Shepherd. In John 10:3 He tells us that one of the functions of the shepherd is to lead the sheep out. That means that, like the shepherds of old who knew where to take the sheep for water and pasture, Jesus knows where to lead us. He knows what lies ahead. We do not know how He will lead us, but we know that He is faithful and trustworthy.

Live generously

> Give portions to seven, yes to eight,
> for you do not know what disaster
> may come upon the land.
>
> (Ecclesiastes 11:2)

Some people tend to turn inward after a time of trial or suffering. Self-pity or bitterness may cause them to withdraw from others. This inwardness may affect us in such a way that we no longer reach out to others. This should not be the case for anyone, but least of all for Christians.

But it may also be the sense of insecurity that is so much part of the aftermath of a traumatic experience. After our own experience, the local gun shops reported a boom in trade.

The word 'portion' in this text alludes to an ancient eastern custom where the host at a feast would distribute special succulent portions of food or delicacies to honoured guests. This is referred to in 2 Samuel 6:19, Nehemiah 8:10 and Esther 9:22. The custom eventually came to mean more than a portion of food. It was broadened to include the generous help one man might extend to another.

The words 'to seven, yes, to eight' is a way of saying 'as many as you are able to help'. This expression is also used in Micah 5:5. Thus we are urged to live generously in this uncertain world with all its risks and to extend help to as many as we are able. Why does the writer of Ecclesiastes suggest this mentality? The answer lies in the next line: 'for you do not know what disaster may come upon the land.' We have no way of predicting the future. Some calamity may rob us not only of our material goods, but also of the ability of doing good with what we possess.

Often when we live unselfishly and generously, God disposes the hearts of others to help us in our need. In other words, this is an Old Testament way of saying what the apostle Paul said in 2 Corinthians 9:6–8:

> Remember this: Whoever sows sparingly will also reap sparingly, and whoever sows generously will also reap generously. Each man should give what he has decided in his heart to give, not reluctantly or under compulsion, for God loves a cheerful giver. And God is able to make all grace abound to you, so that in all things at all times, having all that you need, you will abound in every good work.

Many of you will be familiar with the parable of the shrewd manager which Jesus told in Luke 16:1–9. This parable depicts the way a man who was about to lose his job made provision for his future. He did so by using the authority at his disposal to make people indebted to him. The point that Jesus was making is that we are to use our material possessions for eternal purposes. He puts it this way in Luke 16:9:

> I tell you, use worldly wealth to gain friends
> for yourself, so that when it is gone, you will
> be welcomed into eternal dwellings.

But before Jesus makes this comment, he makes another in verse 8:

> For the people of this world are more shrewd
> in dealing with their own kind than are the
> people of the light.

Sometimes Christians can learn a thing or two from the world. One of the lessons we need to learn is to live for today and to take the opportunities we have each day. I am aware that this is not the whole picture. We are ultimately to live for eternity. But there is a sense in which we can use each day to the full for eternity. One such way is to be generous and open and to resist the temptation to shut everyone out when tragedy comes our way. Live generously and do what you can while you can. Paul's great chapter on generosity contains these words: 'see that you also excel in this grace of giving' (2 Corinthians 8:7).

Don't dwell on what cannot be changed

> If clouds are full of water,
> they pour rain upon the earth.
> Whether a tree falls to the south or to the north,

in the place where it falls, there will it lie.
(Ecclesiastes 11:3)

There are certain things in life which we can do nothing about. Two examples are given here—clouds full of water and trees blown over in the wind. If the cloud is full of water, it will rain. A tree blown down in a storm may fall in a very inconvenient way. These are things we cannot control.

Many people have lifelong struggles over things that happen in their lives which they cannot control or change. Many who have suffered abuse carry feelings of guilt or anger around with them. Others carry real guilt for inflicting harm or damage on someone else. We all have memories we would rather erase. Most people have regrets about things that have happened in the past. Others carry guilt and humiliation for what members of their family have done. I remember a shy young girl who was a member of our youth group. Not many people could get close to her. She had a family member who was convicted for murder and she carried the scars.

We are all tempted to think about the 'might-have-beens'. If only I had not travelled so fast; if only I was five minutes earlier; if only I had not panicked; if only I had not given into that pressure. The list is endless. But the fact is that there is nothing we can do about the past. To put it into the words of the writer of Ecclesiastes, the tree has fallen. It is done and cannot be undone.

We all know that there are many ways in which we can make amends for hurts we have caused, provided the hurt was not too great. But there are occasions when no amends can be made. Likewise, in certain areas of life there are things which cannot be undone. We cannot undo a motor car accident, nor can we undo a terminal illness. Some things run their course. How are we to handle these?

The answer is to stop brooding on the things we cannot change and begin to grapple with the things we can change. We must do what we can about the future. The attack on our church can never be undone. The tree has fallen, but we can pick up the pieces and go forward . We thank God for Christ and His death on Calvary. We can bring our failures and sins to Him, leave them there and go forward.

We thank God for the indwelling Holy Spirit who regenerates us and changes us so that we can overcome the old harmful habits we used to have. We thank God for the throne of grace. We may come to that throne with all our weakness, confusion and need and obtain the help we need day by day. You may have been abused, misused, trampled upon or unfairly treated.

You may have suffered great hurt, trial or tragedy. But what are you going to do about it? Are you going to dwell on it indefinitely? That is a way to failure and sadness. You can however choose another option. You can say, 'The past is the past. I cannot change any of it. But by God's grace I still have a future and I am going to plan for it.' That is the way forward.

Don't make excuses

> Whoever watches the wind will not plant;
> whoever looks at the clouds will not reap.
>
> (Ecclesiastes 11:4)

After a harrowing experience we quite understandably need time out to sort out our feelings and our future. Often the real trauma only sets in three or four months after the event. The strength we seemed to enjoy at first seems to wane and we feel strangely weak, depressed and lonely. In this condition we can develop a mind set that refuses to venture forth again. This may well become a habit or a lifestyle so that some people may always look for excuses not to act.

The text we are looking at uses an agricultural illustration to make this point. The writer talks about planting and reaping. If farmers had to wait for ideal conditions, nothing would ever get done. The same holds true for us. We may have to fight against the feeling that 'we are not ready yet'. It is possible after a while to use this reasoning to cover up our desire to brood over things. It is also possible to enjoy the feeling of self-pity. And so we never feel ready to move forward.

Many people may have a genuine fear of getting back into social circulation after a traumatic event. They may experience extreme nervousness, loss of self-confidence, embarrassment and have a host of other struggles to face. The temptation could well be to do what the procrastinating farmer does—look at the clouds and say, 'The weather does not look good today. No sense planting in this wind or reaping if it is going to rain.'

If we keep waiting for the circumstances to be just right, when will we ever move forward? Some may use circumstances as an excuse to cover up laziness and idleness. Others may use it as an excuse to cover up hidden fears and unresolved issues. The point is that we will never get back to normality until we start doing the ordinary things of life again. Planting and reaping were not unusual activities. They formed part of the ordinary everyday activities of the agricultural life of the nation of Israel.

The way forward is to stop dwelling on what happened and start getting back into the normal routine of life. It is not as if we who are Christians are without divine help. We have God as our Father. We must trust Him and move forward. Nor is it as if we are without friends and helpers. Christians usually have a warm church fellowship who, given half a chance, will be glad to help. Let's stop making excuses. Stop saying that the time is not right. Beware of the temptation of self-pity which says, 'I don't "feel" right yet!' Make a conscious decision to stop making excuses and, however painful it may be at first, begin doing the things that must be done.

You cannot live without risks. You cannot live without relationships with others. You cannot live in the past, and you cannot constantly make excuses about the present and the things that need to be done now. Grasp these things and you are on your way forward.

Accept the mysteries of life

> As you do not know the path of the wind,
> or how the body is formed in a mother's
>   womb,
> so you cannot understand the work of God,
> the Maker of all things.

(Ecclesiastes 11:5)

I have dealt elsewhere in this book with the problem of God's inscrutability—our inability to understand the mind of God. There are people whose brooding over life's tragedies and trials takes the form of dwelling on this very element of mystery. They silently wrestle with the question of why God allows things to happen. There is usually no answer to the question and they sink into increasing bitterness and anger.

This is quite obviously not a way forward but rather a step backwards. Until we come to terms with the fact that we will not understand everything that happens in life, we will constantly struggle within ourselves.

This verse makes clear that there is a realm of the unknowable. It is unknowable to us but obviously not to God. He is the Maker of all things. The writer illustrates the majesty of God's creation from two familiar things which constantly arouse wonder in us—the formation of the human body in the womb and the freedom of the wind. Although modern science has unveiled many of the secrets of nature, these two experiences never cease to amaze us. We always feel a sense of awe before the wondrous fact of the conception, formation and birth of a human being. And we feel a great sense of helplessness and smallness as we witness the great upheavals caused by natural phenomena. God is the Maker of all things. How can we ever hope to understand fully what the writer of Ecclesiastes calls 'the work of God'?

We have no idea what He is doing now or what He plans to do in the future—either with us or with others. We do not know what calamities will come upon the earth (verse 2), what weather He will send (verse 4), or how long we have to live before He summons us into His presence. Because we do not know these things, nor can we possibly know them, we have to accept that there are things a bout which we will always be ignorant. Our duty is to cast off the distractions and fears, commit ourselves into the hands of this powerful, all-wise and good God, and set about the business of living our lives for His glory. We should witness to the gospel of Jesus Christ and His saving grace; pray for those around us and for the world, and do as much good as we can in the years left to us. This is not to be insensitive to those who are grieving over a great loss or struggling with the aftermath of a great tragedy or a unique experience of suffering. But what other option do we have? A wise and loving Father has left instructions for us in His Word.

Our duty is to heed what He says. After all, if He had a hand in allowing the experience, he is surely the one who knows the way out.

Be optimistic and full of faith

> Sow your seed in the morning,
> and at evening let not your hands be idle,
> for you do not know which will succeed,
> whether this or that,
> or whether both will do equally well.
> (Ecclesiastes 11:6)

Here is a call to a buoyancy of spirit and an assurance of faith. Instead of allowing life to beat us down and keep us out of action, we rise above its uncertainties and accept its challenges with faith in God.

Again we have the farmer at work. But this time he is not looking at the wind and the clouds and then dismally assuming that the time is not right. Rather he is full of the joy of the possibilities of a good harvest. He is out in the morning sowing his seed. But more than that. There is still time to do more in the evening.

The sowing simply refers to doing good. It is an Old Testament echo of Paul's words in Ephesians 5:16:

> . . . making the most of every opportunity,
> because the days are evil.

There is a strong note of optimism in this verse which we need to capture in our own lives. God is still our Maker. He is still God and He is our God. All power resides in Him. All is not lost. Life is uncertain and cannot be lived without risks. We do not know what will happen, or when it will happen. But we belong to Him. We are His children and he loves us. There is still a life to live. There are still people to reach. There is much good that can still be done. Let's do what we can. What does it matter if it is not appreciated? We are not doing it for thanks and applause. We are doing it *for Him*.

Among the many things in life of which we are ignorant is the fact that we do not know which of our efforts God may choose to bless. We do not know which will succeed—our efforts in the morning or the evening sowing—or even both. Despite all the bad things that happen, there is also much good. God still blesses us. Yes, there is a Calcutta with its poor and its outcasts. But thank God, there is also a Mother Theresa and her houses of mercy. There are starving millions in Africa and Asia, but thank God there is a *TEAR FUND* and a host of other agencies working practically to show the love of Christ.

Sowing in the morning and in the evening seems to convey not only a spirit of optimism and hope, but also a spirit of generosity to which I have alluded. In 2 Corinthians 9:6 Paul says:

> Remember this: Whoever sows sparingly will
> also reap sparingly, and whoever sows gener-
> ously will also reap generously.

Paul applies this to the matter of Christian giving and urges the same sense of spontaneity, generosity, optimism and faith. All our actions should be accompanied by faith. 'You do not know which will succeed.' The possibility of blessing is always there. 'Whether this or that, or whether both will do equally well.' In other words, God may crown your success beyond your wildest dreams.

We experienced a measure of this after the disaster that struck our church. Once we had dealt with the shock, we realised that God had opened an opportunity for the gospel we would normally never have enjoyed. We therefore began to sow the gospel seed. On radio and TV we tried to relate our experience to the Bible, to God and to the reality of our faith in Christ. Of course our comments were sometimes edited. We had no control over that, but we tried.

The same applied to the newspapers. We released a statement after the event which we knew would be only partially reported in the press . When a large finance house offered to subsidise our entire statement, we put it into all the newspapers we could.

The congregation took every opportunity to witness for Christ. They found a listening ear with almost everyone. Christians were approached by colleagues, friends and family who were not themselves believers. They were asked leading questions. Many Christians around the country had the same experience. At the funeral services and all succeeding services, the gospel was proclaimed simply and directly, and opportunities were given for people to respond.

We tried to sow our seed 'in the morning, and at evening'. We took every opportunity given to us. And the result? At the funeral services alone we had between three and four hundred people respond to the gospel by asking for evangelistic literature and inviting us to help them further. At subsequent services we had scores of people responding each Sunday. We had opportunities to share our faith on Christian radio and TV. Our telephones seldom stopped ringing. We even had strangers making appointments to see us for the sole purpose of receiving Christ as their Saviour. We found ourselves totally overwhelmed with enquirers. It became impossible to follow them up personally, so we devised other ways of making contact with them. I want to stress that an enquirer is not necessarily a convert but we have had the joy of witnessing many true conversions during this time. And what is more, we hear reports from around the country of other churches and individual Christians who are also sharing the joy and excitement of seeing the most unexpected people turn to

God. To God be all the praise and the glory.

Surely this is a time to be busy for God and his gospel. The world is full of religious confusion. It is racked by the devastation of war, violence, crime and corruption. We are surrounded by empty and aching hearts on all sides. We simply must have something to say to them. Therefore we cannot allow ourselves the luxury of withdrawing into our own personal pain and bitterness. We are Christians. We must be different. All is not lost. We have God as our God. We have a great message of hope for our times. We must sow our seed morning and evening.

There will always be someone you can reach for Christ that no one else can reach, a function you can perform for someone that will be a blessing to them. By word, deed, prayer, using telephones, telegrams or a simple dinner party, there are myriads of ways of sowing the seed. Do so, and as you do it believe that God will honour your effort to glorify Him. That is a way forward.

Conclusion

Let's go over the six steps again. Firstly, remember that life is always full of risks. We cannot avoid it. Secondly, try to avoid the trap of withdrawing and shutting yourself off from others. Rather learn to live openly and generously, remembering that one day all opportunity to do good will be gone.

Thirdly, don't fret about things you cannot change. Don't dwell on the past. There is nothing we can do about the things that have happened. If the 'tree has fallen', leave it alone. Your job is to get on with the present and plan as best you can for the future. Remember, fourthly, that in thinking about the future, you should avoid the temptation to procrastinate and make excuses. It is quite understandable that fear, uncertainty and loss of self-confidence will need to be overcome. But overcome it we must. Conditions will never be perfect. We must eventually ignore the 'winds' and the 'clouds' and get on with the business of living normally again.

Fifthly, come to terms with the mysteries of life. God does not always explain His actions to us. We should rather surrender to Him, the Maker of all things, and seek to serve Him faithfully. Finally, we should learn to be happy and optimistic again, giving ourselves wholeheartedly to the task of doing good and sowing gospel seed morning and evening. Life is too short to squander on self-pity. Besides, God may bless our efforts in ways we never imagined and we may bring added joy to our lives by seeing the impact our actions have on others.

Although we are Christians, all mysteries are not answered for us in this world. Like Job, we do not always understand what spiritual dynamics are taking place behind the scenes of our sufferings. But because we are Christians, we know that all things work together for good to those who love God and are called according to His purpose. We know this world is not all we have. It is not our final home. It does not all end six feet below the earth. We have a hope for the future. There is another life waiting for us of which we only get faint gleams now. But it is there.

We are heading for a city whose builder and maker is God. It is a place where at last all tears are wiped away and nothing that can spoil or cause harm can ever enter it. Multitudes are there now awaiting the resurrection day. We wait too. For when our Saviour comes , we know that not only will judgement at last be meted out and Christians vindicated, but it will be the dawn of that day when the shadows will flee for ever. We will enter the city of light and we will reign with Him for ever and ever.

I would like to close this book with the words of a hymn which deserves to be better known than it is. It is simply called 'After':

> After the toil and the heat of the day
> After my troubles are past
> After the sorrows are taken away
> I shall see Jesus at last.
>
> After the heartaches and sighing shall cease
> After the cold winter's blast
> After the conflict comes glorious peace
> I shall see Jesus at last.
>
> He will be waiting for me
> Jesus so kind and so true.
> On His beautiful throne He will welcome
> me home.
> After the day is through.

Bibliography

Atkinson, David. *The Message of Job*. Downers Grove: InterVarsity Press. 1991.

Bridge, William. *A Lifting up for the Downcast*. Carlisle: Banner of Truth. 1979.

Carson, D.A. *A Call to Spiritual Reformation*. Leicester: Inter-Varsity Press. 1992.

'*Diagnostic and Statistical Manual of Mental Disorders*'. American Psychiatric Association.

A Dictionary of Quotations. Edited by Philip Hugh Dalbiac. Nashville: Thomas Nelson Publishers.

Dobson, James. *When God doesn't make sense*. Wheaton: Tyndale House Publishers. 1993.

Dumbrell, William J. *The Faith of Israel*. Leicester: Appollos. 1988.

Great Hymns of Faith. Compiled and edited by John W. Peterson. Grand Rapids: Singspiration Music, Zondervan. 1980.

Haldane, Robert. *An Exposition of the Epistle to the Romans*. Grand Rapids: Evangelical Press. 1958.

Hendricksen, William. *Romans 1—8. New Testament Commentary*. Carlisle: Banner of Truth. 1980.

Kidner, Derek. *The Message of Ecclesiastes. Bible Speaks Today Series*. Downers Grove: InterVarsity Press. 1976.

Kidner, *Derek. The Message of Jeremiah. Bible Speaks Today Series*. Downers Grove: InterVarsity Press. 1978.

Masters, Peter. '*How can we tell the Lord's Disciplines?*'. The Sword and the Trowel. London: Metropolitan Tabernacle. no 3. 1988.

Motyer, Alec. *The Prophecy of Isaiah*. Downers Grove: InterVarsity Press. 1993.

The Oxford Book of Christian Verse. Chosen and edited by Lord David Cecil. Oxford: Oxford University Press. 1965.

The Penguin Dictionary of Modern Humorous Quotations. Compiled by Fred Metcalf. London: Penguin Books. 1987.

Poole, Matthew. *Commentary on the Holy Bible.* Carlisle: Banner of Truth. volume 2. 1962.

Ryle, J.C. *The Upper Room.* Carlisle: Banner of Truth. 1978.

Spurgeon, C.H. *Treasury of David.* Grand Rapids: Baker Book House. Volumes 2, 4. 1977.

Stott, J.R.W. *The Cross of Christ.* Leicester: Inter-Varsity Press. 1986.

Stott, J.R.W. *The Message of 2 Timothy. The Bible Speaks Today Series.* Leicester: Inter-Varsity Press. 1973.

Tada, Joni Erikson and Steve Estes. *A Step Further.* Grand Rapids: Zondervan. 1978.

Van Ness, David. *Crime and its Victims.* Downers Grove: InterVarsity Press. 1986.

Wuest, K.S. *1 Peter. Word Studies in the Greek New Testament.* Grand Rapids: Eerdmans. 1969.